Pothos offers an extraordinarily rich and affecting account of grief, and of how it alters the experiences of love, art, plantlife, technology, friendship, food, illness, protest and crisis. This is a gorgeously messy, passionate book, thrown into disarray by personal loss, and also by the catastrophes of recent history, 'timestamps' of which can be found 'right there singing in the metadata'. Like Frank O'Hara, one of the garrulous spirits invoked by this sociable, choral text, Campbell commits to a way of writing that is 'at least as alive as the vulgar'. *Pothos* opens itself up, again and again, to remind us that it is the 'silly things' which are 'huge & beautiful forever'.
  – **Oli Hazzard**, *Lorem Ipsum*

Utterly contrary to the era of what Philippe Ariès terms 'forbidden death', Campbell's *Pothos* is the most extraordinary book – a meditation on grief that engages with the poetry of Frank O'Hara, houseplants, iPhone notes and the many and multifarious specificities of what it is to be alive and then suddenly without someone. *Pothos* might also be a useful book; in an act of tremendous empathy and generosity Campbell makes her grieving, with all its glittering thinking, deft lyricism and resplendent queerness, communal. If grief, as C.S. Lewis believed, feels like fear then perhaps Campbell's writing feels like courage.
  – **Richard Scott**, *Soho*

Rosa Campbell's beautifully-observed descent into the underworld after her father's death offers the very particular pleasures of intimacy with a stranger, of recognition, of a report from the in-between place of grief, that other world in our world where we might find ourselves at any time, studying longing when we aimed to study the light
  – **Andrea Lawlor**, *Paul Takes the Form of a Mortal Girl*

POTHOS

Campbell

ISBN: 978-1-913642-58-7

Cover illustration by Rosie Robertson - https://www.instagram.com/potted_peach/

Cover design by Aaron Kent

Edited & typeset by Aaron Kent

Broken Sleep Books (2021)

Broken Sleep Books Ltd
Rhydwen,
Talgarreg,
SA44 4HB
Wales

Contents

'I shall offer to the mind all its sorrows, all its mourning garments: this will not be a gentle prescription for healing, but cautery and the knife.'
— *Seneca, De Consolatione ad Helviam*

You who do not discriminate
between the dead and the living, who are, in consequence,
immune to foreshadowing, you may not know
how much terror we bear, the spotted leaf,
the red leaves of the maple falling
even in August, in early darkness: I am responsible
for these vines.
— *Louise Glück, 'Vespers'*

'On one level, I think I have lost "you" only to discover that "I" have gone missing as well.'
— *Judith Butler*

Pothos

Rosa Campbell

i.m. Mike Campbell

You must begin. You must pick a point in time — *before, after* — & simply go from there.

(Everything now is either *before* or *after*.)

Sliding down the dark wood spine between Literary Criticism and Poetry (Anthologies), I sit on the floor of Edinburgh Central Library & get weepy about my dead dad.

It has been almost a year since he died & I am plagued with the feeling that I've done it all wrong — the grief thing. I have refused to read the many books & articles sent by my endlessly kind-hearted friends, I have had no noticeable "stages." On the couple of occasions I've called my mother in tears, she has seemed, frankly, relieved.

I am aware, at least superficially, that there is no right way to grieve, yet this paradigm also seems highly suspect. There are definitely wrong ways to grieve — the ways that make people assholes to those trying to help, the ways that turn you cold, the ways that include self-harm, self-sabotage. Grief can make people vigilantes, it can make them weak, self-centred, self-indulgent. It can make them lash out, panic, career their bikes into pedestrians, dress like idiots. It can make them wild-eyed furies or it can make them wet blanket hermits. It can, most commonly and most egregiously, make them boring.

What a dull, mundane fucking thing it is to be sad about death.

Before the library & the weeping I was in a cemetery, sitting on the tombstone of Jane Lady Lees (d. 17 May 1853) whilst my partner — gently exasperated & resignedly amused — tells me off for being disrespectful. His name is Moss & we are in love. Idiotically, life-ruiningly, giddily in love. In a week we will be 400 miles apart for a while & I will be back to sleeping with my headphones in my ears & sending him photographs of me brushing my teeth. In just under three years we will be rearranging the living room, working out for the second year in a row how to fit a Christmas tree in a tenement flat. In an hour I will be crying silently in the stacks. For now, however, the sun is out & I am trying to get him to kiss me on top of Lady Lees by telling him about Mary Shelley & Percy fucking on her mother's grave. He is googling & saying *allegedly* a lot.

(I think it is perhaps not particularly profound to connect time(s) like this. Proust did it first & did it perfectly well, no need to pick a moment & move around it as if no one has considered the horror of transience before.)

(And yet—
In ten days he will have heard that his friend has died in a climbing accident in Switzerland, & I will be picturing her boyfriend with whom she has been doing long-distance to California & sobbing on FaceTime whilst Moss tells me that it's okay, that he doesn't do that kind of climbing, that he would never leave me. The way I have managed to make it about me is almost shocking; an indication of the kind of grotesquerie I have allowed myself to indulge in just because I lost someone. My compassion has shrivelled & the cycle of grief is unrelenting.)

In the library, I pull books off the shelves almost at random, sliding out something dark green that declares contemporary literature began in 1990. This makes abundant sense to me, as it is also the year I (*tremulous, wavering, lyric "I"*) began. Brought into the world at Leeds General Infirmary on a Wednesday afternoon (weather: Sagittarius sun, Scorpio moon, Gemini rising) by Janie and Mike — as I would call them for the first five years of my life, until I received a sister and they were suddenly transmogrified into *Mummy* and *Daddy*.

December the 12th 1990: I remember my dad claiming that they had timed it so I never had to live under a Thatcher government. I think now, occasionally, about the astonishing number of Tory governments he has not lived under in the past three years.

In the cemetery and the library, though, it has only been about ten months.

POTHOS (disambiguation)

Pothos may refer to:

- **Pothos** (mythology), a character in Greek mythology
- **Pothos** (plant), a genus of plants
  - *Epipremnum aureum*, a plant often grown indoors (formerly grouped within the genus *Pothos* and commonly known as "pothos")
- A statue by **Scopas**

See also:

- **Pathos**

I am on the number 7, or 14, or possibly 49, trundling interminably slowly up Leith Walk, across the Bridges, up towards Nicholson Street and the National Museum, in whose cavernous whiteness sit three people at a meeting that I am late for. I am on the phone to Éadaoín, because I had a date last night and there is Gossip.

and then

I am walking up Chambers Street, telling Éadaoín I have to go, and seeing — as I walk into the misjudged ground-level-of-a-multi-story-car-park-style entrance to the museum — that I've missed a call from my mother. But I'm late and rushing and it can wait.

and then

I am in the balcony café, the clattering of crockery bouncing off the vault, as the business of the meeting (the literary journal that Patrick and I run under the auspices of the university) is pleasantly derailed by Oli's young son, asleep and then awake in his baby carrier.

and then

I am reflexively checking my phone as P says, 'Lunch? Union of Genius? Soup?' & I am saying 'Ah, just give me a sec, I need to call my mum back.'

and then

I am sat at that table, making that phone call, but in the memory I am hovering in the centre of the Grand Gallery, suspended like dinosaur bones for children to stare up at and through.

And then there is a taxi ride & a train journey & a revolving door & my mother's face & a lift with a family looking at us curiously — me with my big pink & purple hiking backpack, my mother's drained face — & a room & a nurse & *twenty minutes ago.*

Let's try again:

My mother says *they say this weekend is critical*

She says *I know you have your party, I thought about waiting to call until after it*

She says *I think you should get on a train*

I say *okay right, should this be right now?*

She says *I think you need to go home & pack & get on a train*

Patrick does not know what to say. I don't even think I've told him that my father has cancer. He has only "had cancer" for about a month and how do you say it anyway?

P says, *okay let's get a taxi, let's call Sean.*

Sean is my flatmate & he somehow appears next to the taxi outside the museum immediately. I don't know how this happens, I don't remember walking down the stairs or anything about the journey except clutching the yellow grab handle with my right hand. I know that at home I moved through thick air. I know that someone else paid for my train tickets because *of course* I had lost my bank card & the replacement hadn't arrived yet.

I don't know how we got to the train station, but I know that at Waverley (more cavernous white space, more clatter & me suspended above the concourse, unbreathing) I couldn't answer questions properly so P ended up panic-buying the largest size of tea at Costa, & that its maroon ridges grew damp & sweaty as me & the train slid between Berwick & Alnmouth & York.

At Leeds, our neighbour Helen picks me up & we drive towards something neither of us know is coming so soon. I don't know the hospital, don't recognise it, still to this day don't know its name. It doesn't matter. All I know is there was a huge revolving door that moved more slowly than I could possibly have believed. And my mother on the other side. And I made a joke.

I didn't know. I knew? I didn't know. Not really. Couldn't have known or else I wouldn't have made it through the revolve. Would have sat down & no one would have been able to revolve in or out. Just me & the door, insistent at my back: *get moving*. But I didn't stop the door, so I didn't know yet, & I made a joke to my mother, who was waiting. Who knew.

She wouldn't tell me how he was, we just got in the lift with Helen and some other people. I remember putting my hands on my knees, crouching down like an athlete after a race, & my huge backpack almost slipping over my head. Someone at some point tried to take it off me, & it got caught on my jacket & I couldn't get free.

It becomes, at some point, impossible to narrativise normally. There's my sister. There's a wooden door, or something that looks like one. There's a room with a couch? Or chairs? Is there a desk? There's a window. There's an influx of visual information.

And then, I suppose, there is death. Waiting in a room in a hospital, already packing its bag, checking to see if there's anything left behind. Because its work was finished twenty minutes before I arrived.

Holly says *no he didn't!*

I sit with my feet up by the window in my parents' room & call Holly & tell her he died & she says *no he didn't!*

Holly says *he didn't!* on a loop in my head, but it's not like Didion. Not magical thinking or denial or unblinking belief or the glitch in your periphery that flashes up their face at the door. No, Holly says *no he didn't!* & I want to laugh.

It's so funny I almost lose all sight of everything.

I have to say *he did!*

Sat on the flat blue cushions on the chest by the window that holds all his jumpers, phone to my ear: *he did! My dad did just die!*

Things happen, and then they are happening and that's almost better somehow. Anticipation is the worst trick humankind ever played on itself — the ability to foretell, to guess at what's around the corner, what could be under the bed.

But when things are happening, you adjust. The world turns on its head & then that's what you're working with, upside-down world.

(Like that thing they say happens with glasses lenses that flip your vision: up/down/down/up, left/right/right/left. In 1950 Professor Theodor Erismann puts goggles on his assistant Ivo Kohler, gives him a cane & turns him out into the mean streets of Innsbruck: *watch what happens next*. Veer left, parry up, hold this teacup, catch this kid's balloon for her. Poor Ivo.

Until! Your eyes simply adjust, up/down/down/up left/right/right/left & you can ride a motorcycle through Innsbruck in your hot new goggles.)

It's August & I'm on Rose Street & my ma calls & tells me they think it's a liver thing. *They've ruled out the really scary stuff* & she's already drawn up a list of foods he should or shouldn't have, to put on the fridge. I can picture it; for my notoriously picky sister endless lists of possible meals were drawn up, & after they came up with "superfoods" my mam had the Guardian's illustrated list of them pinned to the noticeboard for years. I think this new one will be a chart, maybe colour-coded. He's not allowed alcohol ever again & I can't believe I'll never clink a cold glass to his in quite the same way. Can't believe he won't be able to talk about the entirely average local lager on any European holiday as if it was an obscure & sophisticated artisan brew (*I always thought he was such a beer expert, though I still think about the time I told him his beloved classy & continental Stella Artois was known as 'wifebeater' & he stopped buying it*). And then, immediately: adjustments. I picture zero alcohol beer & low sodium foods. I picture the chart on the fridge door. I picture a new normal.

Okay, I think, *that's how it will be.*

I was wrong, of course. He was dead within ten weeks. I have no idea if he ever had another beer. And you have to adjust to that too. We adapt. New goggles. Motorcycle through Innsbruck.

What do you do the morning after? How do you negotiate a world emptied of them?

You will wake up. You will cry, you will get tears in your ears. You will roll over.

Later, you will wash your face. You will stare at your reflection in the bathroom mirror, at the puffy eyes & the soft sleeping t-shirt you borrowed from your sister. You will wear this to bed for the next two weeks & then you will never see it again. It will be in every selfie you take at this time.

You will take selfies, & you will not be able to tell if this is vulgar or not.

You will sit at the kitchen table & you will not be able to work out what to do after that.

Years later (because years will pass, no matter how unbelievable that is), Alexa will ask, 'What did you *do*, those first few weeks? How did you fill your time?' & I will have to look her in the eye, dulled by her own grief & exhaustion & searching for meaning, & say, 'I played a game on my phone where I tapped on hidden objects in a range of animated scenes. I did this for many hours a day, & although I can't remember anything about it now, it brought me a huge amount of satisfaction.'

Life changes in the instant.
You sit down to dinner and life as you know it ends.
writes Joan Didion at the beginning of *The Year of Magical Thinking*.

I had known the end of the world before. I was eighteen &
standing on a platform at Leeds train station & I had just kissed
my girlfriend goodbye so that we could go our (mutual, adult,
sensible) separate ways; her to university, me to interrail
round Europe. When I got on the train I wept & wrote the
words *The end of the world arrived with a kiss* melodramatically
in my shiny spiral-bound notebook.

For months I thought I would maybe spontaneously expire
without her, and to this day there is a brand of deodorant
that puts me in a tiny room in France googling case studies of
animals that have died from separation anxiety.

When my father died it wasn't the end of the world. It wasn't
the end of life as I knew it. Life as I knew it continued —
unbearably normal.

When we got home from the hospital we realised no one had
eaten all day. I have no idea what time it was, but dark outside
in late September. I said I'd make scrambled eggs. If life as I
knew it had ended then they'd be rubbery or I would have
dropped the eggs or they would have got cold as everyone
pushed them round their plates, disinterested in the bodily.

But life was going on, so they were the best scrambled
eggs I've ever made in my life. My mother's best non-stick
saucepan, real butter, fancy salt. As I pushed them around
the pan I already felt guilty for wanting them to be good, for
caring what they tasted like, for repeating to myself Nigella's
advice about low heat & a spatula & long, wide ribbons of
egg — for thinking about anything else.

Reading Didion, I'm glad to know about 'the red cashmere
scarf, the Patagonia windbreaker that had been the crew jacket
on *Up Close & Personal*' that she returns from the hospital to
find, but what I want to ask her is not *what do you do how do
you get through it am I doing it right?* But rather *what were you
about to eat when your husband died at the dinner table?*

I need to know that she remembers, that it matters to her.

I feel sick when she writes that she combined the cash from his pocket with her own. How could she? His money, his items, his life just folded into her own like it hadn't just been next to his body, a part of his personhood. Was it not sacred to her?

When I was going to university (maybe? or travelling, perhaps?), my father gave me a little circular lapel pin with the EU stars on it. He had worn a similar one on every suit jacket I'd ever seen him in, for as long as I can remember. I think for a long time I believed that all suit jackets just came with them in. My pin languished in various cubbyholes in various rooms in various flats for years at university, very occasionally making its way onto the lapel of a blazer when I wanted to make some kind of juvenile assertion of limp political belief. This was long before a sense of Europeanness was a contentious notion — the EU was a boring fact of life, a dull organisation over in Brussels that was part of the fabric of normal political & civilian life in the UK. It was very much not cool for me to wear this pin.

After he died, I put it on my (fake, £20) leather jacket and, imbued with newfound political & sentimental significance, it became quietly talismanic.

The day — maybe eighteen months later — that I found the gold back on the floor under the coathooks, and the tiny dented absence in the jacket's lapel, was perhaps the first time since that room in the hospital that I experienced anything that I could reliably identify as grief.

Grief the way I expected it, grief the paroxysm, grief the wave that drags you under. I found myself frantic, hysterical, tearing coats from the hooks, throwing shoes down the hall, knowing it was gone forever & that I was just going to keep losing piece after piece of him until I had nothing.

When Alice Roosevelt died on Valentine's Day, 1884, Theodore wrote in his meticulously-kept pocket diary, *'The light has gone out of my life.'* He was 25, his wife had just given birth to their daughter, & his mother had died hours earlier from typhoid fever. Above the single sentence he had drawn a large X.

In photographs of the diary you can see entries from the following days showing through the thin paper; the clearest one begins *Alice* but the next word is obscured by the X.

I think of him sitting down at the end of the day, opening the diary as usual & pressing down hard with his nib, scratching out two perfect, grim lines.

A couple of days after my father dies I re-open my diary to sort out the life that I'd unceremoniously dropped back in Edinburgh. I look at the box for Friday the 29th September & put a cross in it. It feels self-conscious & performative, but I think that's why I do it. Sometimes I think that we watch ourselves "grieve" & that's how we understand it.

(I read C.S. Lewis & think *how's that for A Grief Observed, baby*)

Whenever I cry I end up looking in the mirror, drawn weirdly & inevitably to my own reflection. I think I read once that we do that to make our sadness real to ourselves — to bear witness to it: *yes, you are sad, look at those tears, you have made those out of your sadness*. When I was younger I once commented to my mother that crying, at least, made my eyes look a nicer shade of blue. She was unimpressed.

At the end of 'To the Mountains in New York,' Frank O'Hara writes—

> You died, and the tempestuous blue of my eyes
> filled the sails of your funeral barque
> which, I remember, was filled with walnuts.
> It is raining. Shall I grow trees or flowers?

It's an earlyish poem, & not a great one, & he opens it claiming that 'I'm dropping my pastoral pretensions!'

He's not, though. Can't help but end on trees/flowers. Can't help but echo my childish vanity: tempestuous blue.

We love ourselves as sad people — or no, love the idea of our sadness. The image that we could be: pitiable lost soul, teardrop clinging elegantly to a damp eyelash, delicate sniffle.

But O'Hara is smarter than that, knowingly overblows himself, puffing out sails of a walnut-filled funeral barque & summoning life from the ground with the flippancy of choosing an ice-cream flavour. *Shall I grow trees or flowers* he asks the dead.

When I moved to Edinburgh from Liverpool I moved into the spare room of a beautiful sunny little flat on the second floor of a tenement building in Leith. The current tenant, Jen, had lived there for about three or four years with various flatmates & she loved it. Loved Leith, loved the kitchen with its view over the allotments, loved the watercolours her old flatmate had done of that view, loved the vintage dresser in the kitchen covered in half-empty bottles of spirits & semi-ironic votive candles & the fluffy fern that shed its needles everywhere, loved the massive ugly armchair in the box room next to her record player, loved the lamp behind it with its fringed baby-blue shade, loved the white walls & the imposing dark wood furniture she'd filled it with, loved Mr Jungle, the horrific monstera that stretched its creepy aerial roots over both sides of the mug cabinet, loved the giant yucca on the butcher's block, loved the love plant with its heart-shaped leaves that she'd been given by a couple she knew when they moved away, loved having the responsibility of being the care-taker of their love.

I loved it too. I loved who I was going to be in this new place. Mostly, I decided, I was going to be a person who had houseplants. This mattered much more than actually having the houseplants; I simply wanted to be a person who had houseplants. I don't know what that meant to me, necessarily, but I can guess — nurturing, responsible, loving, loved. A creative & a creator: a producer & sustainer of life, a god.

This, then, is what I presumably had at the back of my mind when my mother came up to visit for the first time & bought me, as a flatwarming gift, the first plant I saw — an abundant, fertile-looking thing with fat glossy leaves & a promise from the florist that it would produce vines.

For the first few months I watered it to the point of spillage; the soil growing darkly putrid with saturation, white spots of mould blooming in the murk. I googled & found out it was a pothos & was probably dying of root rot. I panicked for a bit but assumed I'd only quicken its death if I dislodged it from its pot & tried to get involved in its roots. So I left it alone — let it sit at the top of my bookcase & occasionally tipped the undrunk half of my water glass into it, when I remembered. I let it grow long; let the promised vines hang over the front of my books & the side nearest the window. Vaguely watched the leaves curl upwards towards the light & brushed past them to lean out & look at the world.

I got busy; stopped crying in the foyer of the National Library of Scotland, started writing the first chapter of my PhD, sat on hills with friends & sat in pubs with friends & sat in kitchens with friends & finally ended a relationship I should have left in Liverpool.

Jen moved out & my friend Sean moved in. We kept Jen's plants, stewards of them until she found a permanent place in London to take them to. The love-plant didn't seem to mind who its guardian was, which made me think its original owners must still be out there together, their love keeping it alive. The fern went ghostly pale & died, but we kept it on the dresser in the kitchen, the needles a fine dust over all the new half-drunk wine bottles.

The plants were a background thing, while Sean & I pursued lives as full as we could make them: parties, dates, dinners, events. Our policy was to say yes to everything. On an afternoon not long after he moved in, we sat in his half-unpacked room, backs to the wall & legs up against — what? a mattress? the back of bookshelf? some tall blank thing — & were hit simultaneously by the vague but desperate need to be out in the world, to find where the people were, to be *part of it*. We struck out to climb Calton Hill, ended up at a gallery opening & then an odd party I suddenly remembered having been invited to, all the time pushing to make connections, to reach our aerial roots into the ether in the hopes they would hit something nutritious.

It wasn't until much, much later that I realised that Mr Jungle was even a monstera; Jen having let the roots hang down over our kitchen cupboards for so long that I assumed they were weird dead vines, & the two lone leaves having never achieved the glamorous lobes & fenestration that make a cheeseplant so beloved of aspirational instagram accounts.

And it wasn't until after Sean moved out, and Moss moved in, until I looked around at things in the flat that had taken on the immortality & inevitability of backdrop, until after I'd sent a retrospectively humiliating message to an Expert on a plant identification app (*had this for ages but have no idea what it is?? seems to have monstera leaves but the only thing that grows are these long thin brown vine things?*), that I finally realised that what the poor thing needed was someone to take a pair of scissors to its four-foot roots & shove the shorter ends back into the pot, as far into its own soil as possible.

(Two months later, the Expert, Michael: *it's a monstera ;) ;) those are its roots!*)

(Thank you, Michael)

The pothos is not special. It is not symbolically useful, it is not rare, it is not hard to grow or care for. On Wikipedia they recommend them for offices & malls because they tolerate what essentially amounts to neglect. Everyone has one. You know it, it's the nice evergreen one with the trailing vines & the perfect leaves — ur-leaves, heart-shaped & shiny & slipping out of the stems like offerings. Sometimes they're variegated, dappled with bits of sun-bleach, sometimes dark & glossy.

They originally come from Mo'orea in French Polynesia — one of the Windward Islands (this is, at least, an exciting beginning). They grow wild across tropical climates, climbing up trees and whatever else they can find, using aerial roots that cling hard. It has been considered 'invasive' in Sri Lanka, a 'threat' in South Africa. Its entry in the Global Invasive Species Database includes a note that it is '[l]ikely to cause significant ecological or economic harm in Hawaii and on other Pacific Islands.'

As a houseplant, on the other hand, it is invasive only in its ubiquity. It is often called *devil's ivy* because its leaves stay determinedly green even when left in the dark, & it is, delightfully, almost impossible to kill.

When I got back from a two-month research trip to the States, having left my plants in Sean's care, my pothos was dead. Its two vines held little more than three yellowing leaves each, the bare little wounds opposite the root nodes all jagged & vulnerable. It was chronically overwatered, chronically under-encouraged, chronically lonely.

I think it probably needs repotting, he said, shrugging.

[What's the metaphor here?]

[You might well ask.]

[Is my grief the pothos — capable of surviving my neglect? Unloved backdrop scenery?]

[Not quite.]

[More complicated: pothos as projection of sense of self; said selfhood under pressure from Great Changes.]

[Simpler: pothos as death. Everyone has one. Not special.]

[Stupider: pothos as me. Thriving despite it all, baby.]

[Truer: pothos as nice green thing. Pothos as growing thing. Pothos as occasionally chaotic uncontrolled thing. Pothos as nearly dying thing, as revived thing, as cared-for thing, as reason to care.]

[Not quite.]

Somewhere, & I can't find where, Eileen Myles writes (or talks?) about how getting a dog taught them how to look after themself. *If the dog needed water, it was probably because I needed water, if the dog needed to go outside, I probably did too.* Something like that (sorry Eileen). Dog as auxiliary self, as thing to reflect your needs back to you. Rosie as Eileen, Eileen as Dog.

I look back through three years of my Notes app & —

(no word of a lie not that you'll believe this thing I'm writing to be *true* per se anyway but truly I found this & truly I wrote this & truly the timestamps are right there singing in the metadata)

— find on the 3ʳᵈ of May 2017 a poem draft beginning 'I theorise about my parents deaths'; a notion so inconceivable to me on that day that I felt *safe* writing it. Within five months my father was dead.

& now (here it is) the flash of horror that my sick cosmic curiosity somehow *did that*. That I stitched a celestial banner that read

I HAVE NOT BEEN TOUCHED BY DEATH

& something vast & impassive was goaded & inked Susan Sarandon on the reverse singing *touch-a touch-a touch-a touch me* & look what happened.

Later it (somehow) gets worse. I scroll to find *fruit eggs milk tomatoes onions bread maybe salad stuff sweet potato maybe* (13 July 2017); *garam masala deodorant bin bags triple sec oranges* (same day, weirdly); *Stendahl: flaneur as seeing everything (transparent eyeball??)* (4 August 2017); *Mayer/Waldman affair?* (23 August 2017: the day my mother calls while I am all but flying down Rose Street after interviewing Eileen Myles, to say it looks like liver failure so low-sodium & no booze forever!!! & I swerve away from meeting P for drinks at the Book Festival to cry in the basement of my friend's bookshop); *Andre Aciman - Call Me By Your Name* (21 September 2017: E recommends me a book because it features the word 'apricock'); & then there it is, the poem I write on the bleary panic-boredom train to Leeds after I call Holly & Meg & Fred & Claire & anyone I can think of to say the thing that will not tempt fate but allay it (the stupid shield of thinking the thing to stop it from happening, saying the thing to speak it out of being: it does not work it does not work) & that I will later title 'On Taking Selfies When Your Father is Dying' —

My father is barely even hours from death. My father is dying faster than I thought was at all possible. My father is in a hospital room (*the view is really quite nice as these things go* says my mother, days before) being told that I am on my way, that I am on the train. My father is miles away from me & death is on a faster train than I am. My father is conscious? unconscious? drifting between? I don't know (then), I don't know (now, or I have forgotten if I was ever told). My father's hand is being held. My father's arm will stay warm just long enough for me to put both hands on it. My father's arm will have a weird & difficult coldness to it that seems to come from the inside out which is bad & wrong. My father's arm will still have all his freckles & the perennial tan line from his watch strap & I will put both of my clammy awful hands on it & I will be alive & he will be dead.

Nine months later I will be in New York & I will go to the Met Breuer with Moss to see *Like Life: Sculpture, Color, and the Body* on Eileen's recommendation.

The final room will be filled with horizontal figures, variously lounging, prostrate, reclining (one, Philippe Curtius' *Sleeping Beauty*, even *reclining and wiggling* like Frank says of Jean Harlow in 'To the Film Industry in Crisis'; her waxy chest inflating & deflating almost imperceptibly).

I will wind through the plinths & beds, a little disturbed but euphoric *euphoric* at this life I am being allowed to live until —

Paul McCarthy, *Paul Dreaming, Vertical, Horizontal*

& it looks just enough like him that I am suddenly in the stairwell with my hands on my knees while Moss hovers his hands just above my shoulders & asks whether I want to be touched.

(I always want to be touched.)

After the poem the next thing I write in the Notes app is the pseudo-eulogy I give at his funeral (8 October 2017 at 22:49) & then the draft of an apologetic email to my students when I go back to teaching (13 October 2017 at 15:17) & then life comes back proper with *teabags eggs hair dye courgettes Maldon salt* (16 October 2017 at 18:23).

This is why the Notes app is perhaps the truest record I have of all of it — the journal I didn't even realise I was keeping, with all its minutiae & mundanity & its unperformed performance. It's like Holly's *no he didn't!* — blurted out in all its unedited horror, the most reassuring condolence I got.

This is how it actually all happened: I bought eggs & then I had a phone call that changed everything & then I went back to buying eggs. I bought new luxury salt. I still wanted that.

Sure, my heart breaks for the person who wrote *Two pots on the terrace (2016)* and *Garden #3* at the Hockney exhibition on the 21st of May (four months out), who on the 25th of July at 18:29 (two months out) wrote *5' x 3.5'* to remember the dimensions of something to be framed, who on the 9th of September at 11:35 (twenty days out) wrote a three-stanza poem about the mouse who lived (lives?) in the cavity behind her washing machine.

But six weeks after the fact, a new/not-new, remade/selfsame person writes a draft to be submitted to the newly-established & not yet iconic Instagram @_personals_, an account made up of faux-throwback but entirely new-fangled "personals" ads written by & for queers across the globe.

[it will later become the dating app, Lex, because time moves endlessly onwards]

13 November 2017 at 09:11, the morning after burgers with E where they are like *oh my god you have to submit one!* because we are vaguely attempting to do the poly thing (i.e. E has been poly for years & I have a tendency to call it "the poly thing"), I write an ad.

14 December 2017, texts to E:

R: I think I might have found The One
R: from this
R: [screenshot of an Instagram feed]
R: he lives on a BOAT
R: in London
R: [screenshot of a selfie on a canal boat w/ the caption "captain of my ship"]
R: (u can captain my ship any day etc etc)
E: ahahahah i am like omg GOALS at this guy, what a look, what a BOAT

On March 25th, Moss, who hates to fly, takes a propanalol & gets on a plane to Edinburgh, & I walk towards him, lost on Waverley Bridge in the dark.

When Maggie Nelson writes about the way Eileen returns & returns again to the moment(s) of their father's death, she calls it a 'primal scene.' It is archetypal, held in a timeless perpetuity so that Eileen can use it as a talisman of selfhood: *this is my background, this is my trauma, this is who I am.*

For me, though I too return, rewrite, review, reframe, the moments —

(phone call in the vast chasmic whiteness of the National Museum // taxi with Patrick & Sean like bodyguards, me blankly gripping the yellow curve of the handrail // lost bank card & the panic-packing though I do pack for illness & comfort & grief // knowing // massive tea P buys for me at Waverley // forehead banging insistently on the train window // jokes & small talk with Helen in the little car from the station // the revolving door of the hospital, with my mother on the other side // knowing, knowing // my mother on the other side // the clutch at my chest // 'but that's my daddy' // my sister in florals? my baby sister already calmer, having lived with it for twenty minutes // twenty minutes too late // we held his hands // he knew you were coming)

— are not sempiternal but rooted in then-ness. I know what I was wearing because I took a selfie that morning. I know that because it was a particular tight black top it means I was allowing myself to like my body a little. I know who I was sleeping with because I was wearing someone else's scarf, because the selfie was taken on my bed, but I hadn't slept in it. I know me & Sean were supposed to be throwing a party the next evening, & I know who I wanted to show up.

I know who I was because I know who I loved, and who loved me: the phone call to Éadaoín on the bus that meant I missed my mother's first one; how P suggested we get soup after the *Scores* meeting, & I said I just had to quickly call my mother back because my dad was sick (*did I mention?* I hadn't, it had all happened so fast); how Sean told me to wear my big white fisherman's jumper because that's what I needed right now & he was wearing his & he felt like my brother (*o my brother*); how Holly unquestioningly left a meeting to take my call from the train, how when I called her back to say it (*say it, idiot*) she said *no he didn't!* & I loved her for the unrehearsed truth of it.

35

None of this is a primal scene —

(though of course I became positively primordial in the little locked-away room in the ward, which must be built for this kind of news to be broken in, though the nurse said it wasn't soundproof when I asked & apologised after screaming *fuck fuck fuck* in her face)

—& I don't want it to be. I refuse to have it be the essential foundation of my Quite Shit new late-twenties self. It's an excuse. For not writing my PhD, for being less generous with my time, for turning inwards.

A couple of days after I screamed *fuck* in a lovely nurse's face & clutched at my chest & said *but that's my daddy* & got snot all over someone else's beige pashmina, I stood on Ilkley Moor & felt like I finally understood the *wuthering* bit of *Wuthering Heights*. The wind was in me, rushed through a hole in my chest that wasn't really new but felt fresher, fleshier. I don't know if I was crying but I was like Schrödinger's Weeper at that point, always simultaneously sobbing & not, & the rough air in my lungs was like the kind of roaring that I needed to actually *do* but couldn't summon the energy for. Was the weather wuthering? Was I? Not sure. It was wuthering. Wuthering was happening. I decided I needed it to continue wuthering, that that was what was going to keep me feeling alive (which seemed important). I heard people ran for their grief, presumably to achieve the same kind of breathless, gasping, drowning effect.

Running, sadly, is inherently pointless and maliciously boring, so I decided to swim.

At various points over the next few months I managed a degree of peace under the chlorinated skin of the Leith Victoria public pool, pushing steadily through the water & thinking about my body — blessedly, gloriously weightless, for once.

Peace is fucking useless though, and a leisure centre pool does not wuther. I didn't need to float, I needed to drown.

When I got back to Edinburgh I also contacted a perfectly nice boring man with whom I had had a perfectly nice boring date and perfectly nice boring sex the night before my father died. I have no idea whether this was an attempt to, as they say, *feel something*, or to turn back the clock, or perhaps simply do something normal. Maybe I just needed intimacy; for someone who barely knew me to take care of me — not because they felt any obligation, but because even three weeks after I had bailed on a planned second date in order to sob & wuther in Leeds, they still wanted something from me.

I arrived late, having hung around in St Andrews to wait for Sean to also finish a date & drive us back across the Forth. The man didn't seem to mind much. After food there was wine & after wine there was sex & after sex there was gazing. Rather a lot of it, & only in one direction. I shifted a bit & then sat up a bit & laughed nervously a bit & said *so obviously with the kind of place I'm in right now I need to keep things pretty casual* & he began to cry.

& I held him as he sobbed himself to sleep & in the morning I said *I think I'm probably not emotionally stable enough for you right now.*

I bought a large sandwich on the way home & walked across the city shoving bits of escaping tomato into the corners of my full mouth & thought about moving the little cactus from my bedroom windowsill to outside the door of the flat. I had a very hot shower.

It may seem like there's a point about gender & quote-unquote emotional labour here but in many ways the sandwich & the walk & the hot shower are the point.

One of the many useless things about grief is that it is unnecessarily bodily. On the same Ilkley Moor walk where I'd had my wuthering revelation, I also tentatively proffered a thought to my mother & sister: had they, by any chance, noticed they were shitting more? Grief, it seemed, had gone straight to my bowels.

There's something no one tells you. There's something the cards & nice messages don't mention.

My mother stopped eating. Just lost interest in food for a few months. My sister disappeared into the softest fabrics she could find, submerged in fleecy dressing gown & fluffy blankets except for the smallest necessary section of her face: little mouth, bunged up nostrils, eyes trained on Attenborough documentaries.

I, upon returning from the family home, had occasionally grim, mildly violent, ill-advised sex with people whom I vaguely wanted to treat me badly, drank a fair quantity of red wine, bought a lip stain, took hot showers.

I began to find it astonishing how easy such methods of fleeting intimacy were, once I'd relaxed my grip on it all. Anxiety about relating to others seemed to melt away — who cared? The line between friendship & sex gave way to slippage; I didn't want to talk, I didn't have any feelings to speak of. Suddenly I was just a *thing*, moving through space, moving through the city. *Don't stop.* I could just leave the next morning, buy a fancy coffee & be alone with my body in the early light on the Meadows; boots in dew & boots in mud & tired thighs & the first cheese twists from the bakery section of Sainsbury's & my steamed-up bathroom & the leggy kalanchoe on the cistern that I always thought probably enjoyed the tropical environs & finally my own untrammelled bed.

There's an episode of *Buffy* in which Buffy's mother has a brain tumour & is about to die. Dawn, little sister of the Slayer, gets taken away from the hospital to sit by a carousel & eat ice cream. It doesn't solve anything but — she says — 'it's better...this is better.'

Buffy, all burnished gold waves, hunts solutions. She's antsy, desperate to fight any proxy for the cancer. That's how she's always won out, before. Kill the Big Bad. This season it's Glory, demon with golden hair to rival the Slayer's own, but as Xander — otherwise pointless — points out, 'Buffy, this chick *creamed* you last time.'

Buffy says she's ready this time, but it's there, I see it hanging from the flimsy rafters, from the boom: Buffy *wants* to get creamed. You can see it the whole way through the bloodless fight scene that follows — our hero, desperate to have the wind knocked out of her. Desperate to drown.

When people started finding out (partly because Sean had to send out an explanatory de-invitation to everyone who was going to come to the party), the messages came flooding in. I simultaneously resented & needed them because they meant it was real & really bad.

They say there are stages. (They say it a lot.)

denial / anger / bargaining / depression / acceptance

I briefly had a therapist, and she told me they don't always follow on from one another, that a person can return & return to stages, or cycle through them in different orders, which sounded a lot to me like someone looked at the whole range of normal human emotion & pretended to codify it.

Maybe I was malingering at the street corner of a particular stage, but the only one I remember is anger.

I spent at least six months incandescent with rage.

It bloomed like hot oil in the dark pits of me. A meat hook, an inverted question mark, a coil of fury, thick in the base of my stomach.

My mother was angry that it had all been allowed to happen so fast. That things got missed in misdiagnoses; that they didn't have time to say things. (I don't know what things. I don't want to think of what things they might not have had a chance to say to each other.)

She was angry that we didn't know in time to get me there. That I wasn't there to hold his hand as well.

[My sister, in a brief and wholly uncharacteristic flash of fury — once, & once only: *I'll never be able to unsee that, though.*]

[She was 22. My little sister.]

The meat hook in me wasn't to be brandished at the fates, however. I wasn't interested in knowing how it had happened (it didn't matter, it didn't matter) or even being angry that it had. Instead, my rage was directed repeatedly, capriciously, violently, haphazardly, coldly & viciously at gentle people saying gentle words.

Every kindness, every sympathy, every *fucking* condolence catalysed, in the grim crucible of my abdomen, a fury that manifested as curled-lip whiplash biting cruelty. Sometimes I could hold this in, or could marshall it towards sarcasm at my own expense ("don't worry, I might be able to be a serious poet now I have a dead dad")

(a round of flinches for the pub table, nobody can meet my eye

—but they let you get away with it, you can say anything when you're grieving, *no wrong way no wrong way*—)

or simply towards gritted teeth, a set jaw.

Sometimes it spilled over: caustic, toxic.

My friend's flatmate, sweet & generous & grief-softened, heard & sent a message:

My heart breaks for you. I lost my own dad two years ago, in the middle of my PhD – if you need someone to talk to in the coming weeks and months, I have been there. I am totally available to talk about leave of absences and other university related stuff, or just to chat about how one carries on.

Tight chest, flared nostrils, balled fist. I almost broke the screen of my phone, drafting—

I will never "need" to talk to anyone about this, as I am not fucking pathetic. I will especially not need to talk about a leave of absence, because I am not weak, and therefore will not need one.

(I deleted it, of course, but I never responded.)

Didion writes that in grief, 'we are repeatedly left [...] with no further focus than ourselves, a source from which self-pity naturally flows.'

No, Joan.

She's wrong about this because she's writing about losing her husband & being lonely. I was single when my dad died, a month fresh into it. A breakup that dims & dips under the tide, obliterated by what came after. Me: frankly buoyant. For a bit.

Being alone didn't mean I was lonely, being alone meant I could be unseen. Grief is only real when perceived, as far as I can tell, which is why I didn't give in to it until I met Moss. Until then there was no one to perform it for. My self-pity only began to naturally flow once it had an estuary as well as a source.

Even looking at my sister's boyfriend, holding her hand on the front row in the crematorium, I felt profoundly glad to be single. To be untethered, free to spring from my seat on the last chord of Nick Cave & the Bad Seeds —

[my mother's somewhat surprising choice, in a strange nod to the Catholic upbringing he shrugged off at 18, to the sacred secularity of it all, to the Northern Irish family in the pews: *I don't believe in an interventionist God / But I know, darling, that you do*]

— & storm down the aisle, past the blur of affected faces, the practiced pity of the attendant, the bowl of flowers I nearly knocked over, & out into the feathery cold.

[Porochista Khakpour sits in an Edinburgh bookshop & says of Joan Didion, *I love her, but she's just like this cold WASP, and everyone around her dies!*]

Even more, back in Edinburgh. No one to self-monitor for, no one to ask too much of, no one (thank *god)* to *process* with. Just me & the feathery cold & the pressing on.

Three months on, a letter from my ex. A rekindling attempt like a guttering flame from a 50p plastic lighter. (Me with my damp, cold wick.)

Many paragraphs recounting time spent having rebound sex across the mythical vastness of Baudrillard's America, before being rudely interrupted:

And then your dad died. I wish I could say that I wanted to run to the airport and book the first plane back to be with you —

I didn't know what I could have done for you. I was never good at comforting you even after trivial things, and have never been around someone who's endured such a loss — and while it's awful to say, it was almost a terrible relief to be so distant. Of course, I wanted to hold you —

I thought it was better for me to be there for you from several thousand miles away.

(Works for me, pal.)

A terrible relief to be so distant.

We don't even like the word — *dead*. It's vulgar, we flinch away from it instinctively, especially when spoken. So flattening, so final, so — somehow — embarrassing.

For some reason this is more true of *dead* than *died*. If I say 'my dad died,' I get the sympathetic crumple of the face, the head tilt to the side, the small release of kind breathy noises. If I say 'my dad is dead,' people don't know where to look, as if I've said something faintly inappropriate, or gauche. The past is okay, it's something that happened to you, a difficult time you got through, a vulnerability you're sharing. The present is horrifying: that people who have died remain dead. Present tense forever.

Philippe Ariès argues that in the early twentieth century, western attitudes towards death underwent a fundamental shift. Before then, mourning was communal — public, even. Bodies were displayed and visited and talked to, houses were opened to all and sundry, and the home was the site of both death and grief. Those left behind wore black for months, constantly displaying their loss, their public status as bereaved. Grief was open, a raw wound, fresh and fleshy and exposed. And then (says Ariès) came the era of 'forbidden death.' Whisked out of sight, death — and bodies, in particular — became private, clinical, hidden away at the end of hospital corridors, a closed door, *immediate family only*. Due to modern medicine, even the "moment" of death became obscured: machines, tubes, monitors.

I can't tell whether Ariès is criticising this change or simply remarking, with requisite scholarly detachment, on the strange and fascinating things humanity gets up to. All I know is that I couldn't comprehend the coffin when the undertakers arrived at our house. It seemed too absurd a thing to look directly at. When we were instructed (gently, gently) to follow it into the crematorium — in front of all these people in smart black wool, stricken faces, a moustache so loud that it seemed to be screaming — I was almost sick with rage.

My friends joke that my face is completely incapable of hiding my feelings. They say they watch me at poetry readings, can always tell when I hate the work. At particularly bad ones they can't look at me for fear they'll erupt with laughter. I can only imagine what my face looked like when the nice undertakers told me to follow the coffin into the crematorium: jaw set, nostrils flared, head shaking like a massive CGI dragon, smoke everywhere. The very picture of a child of Forbidden Death.

I've always hated audience participation.

"Breathe easier! NASA includes golden pothos on a list of recommended plants for air purification. While researching the best greenery to bring aboard space missions, golden pothos was found to effectively remove formaldehyde, xylene and benzene from the air."

I get up every morning after the 29th of September 2017 and my father is dead.

I stare at the coffee table & think about polish and my father is dead.

I see a boat called *Onion Bargee* on the Leeds-Liverpool canal and cannot point it out to my father, who would have enjoyed it, because he died two days ago, and remains dead.

I think about dying my hair pink and my father is dead.

The wind pushes itself through the red leaves on the bush at the back of my mother's garden and my father is dead.

I go back to Edinburgh & the sky is perfect and my father is dead.

I get a new bookcase to put under my window & my room looks different & my father, who is dead, will never know.

I buy new shoes & go swimming & make endless fried eggs & take vitamins and my father is dead.

I spend Sundays in Portobello with Bella, walking along the prom & taking photos of the sea, & going to the live sessions at the Dalriada. I think: I wish my dad could visit & I could bring him here for a pint. I can't, because he is dead.

I hold my friend's new puppy a little too tightly, probably because my father is dead.

I make a very good joke about Louis MacNeice and The Kinks at a faculty curry night and my father — who definitely wouldn't get it — is dead.

I go to my sister's graduation and it is extremely hard because we're very proud of her and my father, who probably would have been the proudest of all, is dead. I take hundreds of Boomerangs of my sister & her boyfriend throwing their caps into the air. My father, who is dead, would have thought Boomerangs were amazing, if confusing.

I throw parties & go to parties & go on strike & get ill & see Hamilton & take baths & fall in love & teach students born after the millennium & finish my PhD & have two bouts of emergency surgery & start wearing lipstick & walk around Pilrig Park & walk around Hyde Park (Leeds) & walk around Kew Gardens & walk around Central Park & walk 120 blocks from the East Village to Harlem & write silly little poems and throughout it all my father, who just would have liked to hear about it, is dead.

I water the plants & repot the plants & buy new plants & move the plants around the flat & turn 28 & 29 & 30 and for the first time in my life the birthday cards only have a message on one side.

(Because my father, you see, is dead.)

On the morning after our first date, Moss & I climb Arthur's Seat. It's a pretty hot day, for March, & I am sweating & desperate to show that I am fitter than I actually am. Trying to keep up.

We get to a top that is not the top, some kind of hillock on the side that looks over the old town & a bit of Leith, & sit down near the gorse. The sky is clean duck-egg blue & I tell him about my favourite colour, International Klein Blue, & Yves Klein declaring the sky his first artwork. I look up at this unbelievable day & decide to claim it too. I tell Moss he can have the land, if he wants.

He laughs at me & we talk more about Klein & abstraction & I lean my head on his shoulder & think: *this is it, I reckon.*

When I was at university, my ex & I went interrailing; blew our student loans on ten days in Poland, France, Italy, Austria. Halfway through the trip, we lost one of the SD cards we were storing photos on. Panicked, I insisted we drew from memory all the pictures we had lost. Ten pages of horrible little sketches (*me with red liquorice hanging out of my mouth in a narrow street, you, baby-faced, in front of the Wawel dragon*), and I still don't really remember anything from Warsaw; my brain seems hardwired to forget anything there is not proof of.

So one of my greatest fears is that the photographs I have of my father are the only images I will be able to hold on to. Only those moments will exist, only that version of him.

Everyone says it, but you don't regret taking a single picture — you only wish there were more.

Moss snuffles & shuffles his way into the bright midday kitchen, the collar on his faded red jumper flipped up on one side like when a dog pricks up just one of its ears in order to gaze at you inquisitively. I've never realised before, but the jumper is a sort of polo-shirt/sweater combo, & is very odd & old-fashioned. I have loved it instinctively probably for this reason. It occurs to me that late '80s & early '90s fashion looks timeless to me because all my childhood photos feature it; the puffy shapelessness of jackets & jumpers still recovering from the shoulder pad era, the washed-out neons (sharp teal, Barbie pink, a particularly bereft shade of violet), the abstract patterning, navy sundresses with buttons all the way down, statement costume jewellery, early athleisurewear before it became sleek & stretchy & yoga-y.

What Moss' jumper says to me is: take a photograph & one day you will have children to look at it.

(I take a photo.)

He has emerged from our room in order to make chicken soup; we are both big believers in mildly old-wivesy methods of healing. Earlier I made a vat of ginger & lemon & turmeric tea, straining it through a plastic sieve into a slightly bleak-looking white teapot that my old flatmate must have left behind. I had instructed Moss to add his own honey & drink the lot, which he won't have done, but I reckon just having it next to the bed like some kind of vaporous potion will have done half the job. He passes me carrot sticks left over from the soffrito & tells me he's been reading Walter Benjamin — the only person in the world to turn to German critical theory as a balm in their sickbed.

(I take another photo, thinking: *there will never be enough photos*.)

(There is a horror in writing about love, particularly in the present tense, because it makes the blind, unbreathing assumption that the present tense will last forever. *Moss & I are in love.* Love suspended in amber, always already, present continuous.)

In hard times, in times where I have felt less myself or less sure of what constitutes the thing I call my self, I find myself returning to the same image: life as a stick of rock. *No matter where you slice it, the same!* The static self, the self that can be said to occupy the space "[insert name here]," running all the way through.

This image was mainly a way of getting through break-ups, of dealing with that neurotic queer need to remain friends with my exes — and the fact of that need not always being fulfilled. It seems likely that the stick of rock, bulwark against the linear trajectory of life, comes from an inability, on my part, to deal properly with loss. I don't want to process, I don't want to *move on*, I want to carry utterly everything with me, utterly all the time.

The second bit of those deservedly enduring E. E. Cummings lines, *i carry your heart with me(i carry it in / my heart)*, is the slightly more desperate *i am never without it(anywhere.*

Amongst the attendees at my maternal grandmother's funeral were some of the careworkers from the Home in which she had spent her final few months. There was much commenting on how sweet this was, how kind it was for them to have taken the time to come when they must look after so many people, must watch so many people die. It's not that that wasn't true, that they weren't good, kind people, but what a thing! to have these people you barely knew at all (& who certainly did not know you — after all, Nana was hardly herself in those last few months) come to this marking ceremony for your whole life.

I am terrified by the idea of being defined by the end-point of my life. Instead, bring to my funeral representatives from every era. Bring me my exes to offer flowers to my widow/er. Bring me all the flatmates that I never texted after we moved out. Bring me everyone who has ever written me a birthday card, shared my bathwater, brushed my hair, bought me a pint. Bring me everyone who can remember the colour of my eyes.

Somewhere in the sharp, cold, nervy haze of my father's funeral, I was struck by the thought that his ex-wife wasn't there.

When Grandpa — my dad's dad — died at the age of 94, having managed to live 9 years without Grandma, still in his own home on the Wirral, it was, all things considered, okay. A good death, as they say, after a long life. Kept his mind until the end, believed simply and entirely in a better place to come.

My dad was an only child, and had sailed his parents' ship of expectations magnificently. The ex-wife, the rejected faith, the lack of marriage with my mother — these things seemed to slip quietly and deliberately out of their minds. Instead: academic and financial success beyond their loftiest imaginings, a brilliant, capable partner (it helped that she happened to be an excellent cook), two perfect children, proffered forth as granddaughters. The impression I got — separated, perhaps, from more difficult conversations — was that he could do no wrong. He was their shining boy.

The shining boy organised his father's funeral almost single-handedly. A full Catholic Mass, the only one I've ever attended, with the Northern Irish family descending on Liverpool to sit on either side of the long, wide aisle. My dad's cousin Patricia sang a Gaelic lament from the gantry, her delicate — and then full-throated — mezzosoprano dropping onto us from high above. During Communion, we (my mother, my sister, me) stood with our hands across our breasts to signify that we were graceless, unbelievers, heathens, and received what I felt to be a patronising blessing from the priest. I remember there being some discussion prior to this about whether my father should take Communion or not, deeply lapsed as he was. I wish I could remember whether he did. The front pew felt like some kind of exposed promontory; the four of us a lighthouse, watched carefully for signs of light. I wondered idly if the Protestant members of the family, from my Grandma's side of Portadown, were seeing us as fellow travellers. Or maybe everyone else was thinking about my Grandpa.

After the funeral, which was affecting but not sorrowful, the extended family had dinner at a pub. Approaching the long table, booked in advance for 14, we were all attempting to negotiate the boundary between appropriate sobriety and a kind of relief, buoyed by curiosity of one another. There was a certain amount of hovering, of who-should-sit-where fumbling, of drinks being plonked and then moved and then plonked again, staking claims. I ended up between my Great Aunt Celine and my sister, with my mother and Patricia across from us, my dad a few seats down. Someone remarked that we'd ended up with all the women at one end, all the men at the other, and someone else joked — hesitantly — that *we should have done what they do at school: boy-girl-boy-girl.*

And my dad, high on things having gone *as well as they could have*, on it being over, on having done his filial duty, on laying things to rest, on a few sips of his pint, says: *or we could really push the boat out and sit Protestant-Catholic-Protestant-Catholic.*

There is an almighty pause — and then, everyone, grateful with laughter.

Later, over her parsimonious bowl of soup, Great Aunt Celine will put her face right up to my left ear, and talk to me about the Troubles, about kneecaps and crucifixion and her sons. There is so much horror and loss in everything she says and yet — at 89 — she is matter-of-fact, even jolly, and is most animated when she asks if I want to get married one day. I say something banal about being *married to the PhD ha ha*, and she says conspiratorially, *ah, sensible, after I got married I was pregnant so often I only had one period.* I almost choke as she blithely continues, *once you start having children, you just can't stop.*

Patricia, from across the table, lets out a scandalised *Mummy!*

No one knew we'd see the Northern Irish family again so soon. That they'd be flying over for yet another funeral (yet another father) less than a year later. Not a good death, this time, & not a long enough life.

& only me, eldest child, to sit in his place, speak from the front, make the jokes.

[THE FUNERAL]

It wasn't really even [A FUNERAL], the way [A FUNERAL] so often isn't. A celebration of (a) life, a slideshow of photographs, donations in lieu of flowers, things in lieu of other things, a sad party in lieu of a person.

The first bit, the crematorium, felt like [A FUNERAL]; the stupid [FUNERAL] car driving my old bus route to school (they do the first bit slow & then speed up so as not to cause traffic on Otley Road). Arriving to all these *people* waiting outside. Furious with all of them.

(Except for Paddy, who arrives with his husband Michael & is *hit* with the full force of me & my sister. Paddy, who's known us since my sister was born, who babysat for us, who laughed at me when I went through a phase of refusing to drink from the *pink* plastic cup, who laughed at me more when I subsequently went through a pink phase, who taught me about what it is to have queer elders, who loved us & our stupid dog & who — I realise in the moment of that hug — is everything to us.)

& then it's [A FUNERAL] with a nice humanist celebrant from Hebden Bridge & *Ode to Joy* (the Anthem to Europe) ringing out from the off-white walls of this presentable, serviceable box.

& the [FUNERAL] keeps going, in the community centre that was once my beloved primary school. I stand on a spot where once, clutching a bright plastic tray, I would have waited to collect a hot lunch, and I read out something like a eulogy, something like a poem. I talked about how we took after him, me & my sister. Even in standing there, I took after him, I suppose. He was always a brilliant public speaker, asked constantly to conferences, casual & approachable but a classic wonk, the ideal keynote. I don't have his same ease, but I don't remember feeling nervous that day. I don't remember feeling much at all. I spoke. I sat down again. The [FUNERAL] continued.

The rest of the [FUNERAL] passes in ways I can't grasp at. Not because of *time* or *memory* (though of course I am endlessly made foolish by them), but because I am at once in my element & yet that element constantly congeals & reconstitutes itself like cold/hot soup.

Ascendant in Gemini: the communicator, moving like a shark through kind faces like so much chum.

In the projected slideshow, a photograph of the family & my ex-girlfriend. Some Catholic relatives ask who she is: I tell, breezily, & swim away as they draw back as if bitten. I keep going, showing teeth left & right. A woman I don't recognise holds my face in her hands, tells me she was one of my dad's students, that he was the best teacher she ever had, that I look just like him. My mother says later: oh god, *her*, I think she had a crush on him. This does not seem like a thing that can be held in fins. It slips. It seems like something you would say about an alive person.

It is a good [FUNERAL]; we know because people keep saying so.

For Frank, death is yellow. In 'Entombment,' he describes how 'the yellow hearses arrive, laden / with nails and pikestaffs for decoration,' all dreamlike grotesquery until the 'cocks drop off' the gargoyles: 'They cry.' The garish nightmare of death. 'Song of Ending' is softer, Berdie Burger (Larry Rivers' mother-in-law) greeted by 'the fragile saffron wings / of death' — a bright elegy in place of a dirge.

And my favourite: 'The Holy Ghost appears to Wystan in Schrafft's / to me in the San Remo / wearing a yellow sweater.'

Oh god Frank let me come for a walk with you 'among the hum-colored / cabs.' You can think about Bunny, I can think about my dad, just a step away, & we can look at the 'yellow helmets' of the construction guys & you can say, 'But is the / earth as full as life was full, of them?' & I can say *I don't know*. I don't know.

'A glass of papaya juice / and back to work.'

Okay. Okay.

Every theory about grief has been utterly uninteresting to me (*our lady of perpetual disdain*), yet, to my horror, one that I saw briefly in a tweet has been asserting itself & its utility repeatedly:

There is a box (a square, if you don't feel like you can exist in that many dimensions right now). There is a button on the inside of the box. Anywhere. There is a ball in the box (a circle if you're fragile). The ball is grief. Death happens & the ball is very large, filling the box like a big cat that loves small spaces. The ball pushes up against the button constantly. The button is, I suppose, pain — or something like it. Perhaps the button is your heart, or your consciousness, or your gut. It's not a perfect analogy. As time goes on — the theory promises, promises — the ball will get smaller. But (*aha!*) the ball is like the bouncing logo from DVD player screensavers of the early 2000s; the one that you kept expecting to hit the corner perfectly so you could shudder slightly in satisfaction. Except the ball does not conform to any kind of pattern, it does whatever the fuck it wants, bouncing around the box on varying trajectories & at varying speeds, & yes — yes it hits the button at random & whenever it feels like it. & at the beginning it's still taking up a lot of space so it's pushing up against the button all the time & everywhere you turn there are things that hurt. Turn— & *whack* the ball hits your diaphragm & you can't really breathe or the ball hits the side of your face & your tear ducts are rent open, may never close. &— etc, etc. As time goes on, *so the theory goes*, the ball will get smaller & so it will hit the button less frequently, but — & here's the kicker, folks — with no less force. Each time the button is pushed, the button is pushed. The button cannot be pushed gently, it cannot be delicately grazed. It is pushed or, I suppose, the ball misses it completely.

The tweet was shorter, I'll admit. But in other words, as time goes on, the debilitating moments, the convulsions of grief get less frequent, but no more predictable, & no less painful. You will feel grief less frequently, but when you feel it, it will feel like nothing has changed. Because, of course, nothing has changed. They are still dead. They will always be dead.

What the theory doesn't cover, however, is a Scorpio-moon-induced — or possibly neurotic — need for control.

Control is the foundation of almost every interaction I have with the universe. So when I feel "sad," I walk down the narrow hallway from bedroom to bathroom, lock the door & grip the sides of the sink until my knuckles turn white. Here I stare into the mirror & silently scream. Looking back: pink blotches like welts, bloodshot eyes, upper lip slick with snot, grotesque contortions of the face.

And then: I stop.

I simply take it all back in. It's like rewinding a tape — I can almost see the tears sucked back up by the ducts. Disgusting, really. The blotchy skin settles itself, the blood vessels in my eyes un-pop, the scream is suddenly a faintly ridiculous memory.

Thanks to this tendency to find a mirror when I am crying—

(or is it that the mirror encourages it? once again: *A Grief Observed*, says Lewis, *…is a grief conjured*, says I)

—I have watched myself time & time again physically swallow moments of grief, eating it like some kind of terrible sea monster. Scylla pulling ships into the vortex of her rage, the terrible calm when the sea smooths out again after the carnage. The grim suck-pop of the last dregs of water going down the bathtub drain. *Nothing to see here!*

So there's the ball deflated. Fuck you, ball.

But control runs both ways, and a few months after he died, I chose to fling the ball at the button.

On my phone, I knew, was a voicemail message, maybe a year old, saved by the strange and capricious O2 gods. It had been left by my dad after a Springsteen concert in Manchester; a huge arena gig that I — living in Liverpool at the time — had gone to with my then-partner, whilst my dad took a train from Leeds to sit in the stands. We didn't actually see each other, just called and texted before the show started, me waving frantically from the middle of the crowd in the hope he could see me.

The gig had been something of an out-of-body experience for me, because I'd been suffering from a horrendous UTI for days beforehand and was dreading the possibility that I would spend 3-4 hours standing in the middle of the Etihad Stadium feeling like my bladder was going to burst. But there in the rain as Bruce played perfect hit after perfect hit, and almost every song from *The River*, never stopping, it was as though I transcended — felt nothing below my midriff, not my aching feet or stabbing pains in my abdomen, just something vast and watery lifting me up. (When I got home, my UTI had cleared up.)

After the gig, we poured out of the stadium, and my ex and I bought huge knock-off tour t-shirts. I thought about buying one for my dad, but didn't. I don't remember when I saw that he'd called and left a message. I think I maybe called him back from the train, but I don't know.

After he died I went through sporadic but intense periods of seeking out his image; the vestiges of his personhood dug out from photographs, constantly googling his name.

There were so few traces of his voice. I rooted out 6 second clips from videos I'd taken one summer in Cornwall that were mostly made up of unflattering close-ups of my increasingly annoyed 17 year old sister; strained to hear the background noise of his conversation with my mother.

'It's the tower house where DH Lawrence lived,' she says.
'Is it?'
'And it's got this very beautiful garden.'
'Yes, I remember.'

It was on one of these recovery deep-dives that I remembered the voicemail. Unusual, because it was my mother who normally called; my dad preferred emails, texts, the occasional Twitter DM. So I remembered it, sitting there in the list. I scrolled, hit play, listened. I think he spoke about the concert, about the fact he was headed back to the train, about the crowds. It was short, & I wept & wept, wishing I could call him back. Ball hits button, bam.

But I can't say exactly what the message said, because as soon as I listened to it, it was gone. As if in listening, I'd alerted some algorithm to its presence, & they swiped it away.

And now, I go to check his Twitter timeline & the account is gone, & I check my texts & I never replied to his last one asking how the Yorkshire puddings made to my mum's recipe turned out & the ball, smaller now, goes slam slam slam slam slam slam.

Here's *Mrs Dalloway*, & here's Septimus Warren Smith, walking in Regent's Park with Rezia. And here (just a step away) is Evans, whom Septimus loves, and who is dead.

'[W]hen Evans was killed,' *writes Woolf*, 'just before the Armistice, in Italy, Septimus, far from showing any emotion or recognising that here was the end of a friendship, congratulated himself upon feeling very little and very reasonably.'

Suck it up, Scylla.

For almost a year I couldn't listen to music. Or, should I say, music with substance. I could only eat candy floss music: relentlessly upbeat, fluffy wisps of 3-minute harmlessness. Nothing that would provide the smallest tug at the heartstrings, nothing that would open the floodgates even an inch. I could not tap into any emotion that wasn't flippant; I knew that one wrong chord, & I'd lose it. Not an option.

Anything I associated with him disappeared into a Spotify playlist called *Vati* that may as well have been a blacklist. Simon & Garfunkel: banned, the Tom Robinson Band: banned, Shania Twain: banned, The Eurythmics & The Byrds & Dusty Springfield & The Kinks & 'Build Me Up Buttercup' by The Foundations, which we couldn't listen to without him telling the story of being at university in Sheffield trying to record it onto (reel-to-reel?) tape off the radio & getting the dinner bell in it. Does that even make sense? Was it just the radio talk trapped in the recording? Who knows, but into the blacklist it went.

I told myself this was a playlist I would listen to in order to help me remember him, but in three years I have never been able to hit play.

Also banned: classical music (too many strings), anything slow (too much space), anything in a minor key, anything with a key change, anything where the singer's voice cracks.

Springsteen was hard. Too large a part of my diet to wholly give up, too painful to swallow. I stuck to newer releases, or the greatest hits, less fraught with individual feeling. But still his voice too often became my dad's (out of tune), too often summoned images of drumming on the steering wheel, the noise I didn't know I thought of as belonging, copyright, to my father. Too often I felt myself in a crowd, surrounded by men who looked like my dad, clutching my standing ticket & knowing he was scanning for me from the seats.

I think now: was this denial? I always thought I skipped straight to anger & stayed there, an eternal flame (another one for the blacklist). But perhaps listening to nothing but Carly Rae Jepsen for months on end is its own kind of refusal.

Chimamanda Ngozi Adichie puts her grief in *The New Yorker*. She writes about the need to stay in the shallows of her own mind; 'a refuge, this denial, this refusal to look.' It felt like that to me: a place of safety, where the music couldn't reach me & I could keep going.

Freud, in 'Mourning and Melancholia,' says it is worth noting that 'although mourning involves grave departures from the normal attitude to life, it never occurs to us to regard it as a pathological condition and to refer it to medical treatment. We rely on its being overcome after a certain lapse of time, and we look upon any interference with it as useless or even harmful.'

It's the ones I stop paying attention to that seem to do best. The sudden virile leaf dwarfing the original cutting; the weird succulent next to the keys in the darkest part of the hall; the blueberry bush from the Midl of Lidl that behind my back produces white flowers like tiny Anne-of-Green-Gables puffed sleeves.

On the day of the one-year anniversary, I sit at the desk in my bedroom in my parents' house, looking out over the back garden that is my mother's pride & joy. I have recently begun calling it my mother's house, but it still sounds stupid, as if my parents are separated & my father's house is somewhere else. A tiny little betrayal, a small erasure.

The bedroom is mostly very similar to how it was for the fifteen years I was in full-time occupation: white walls with aquamarine skirting; cream carpet that I remember picking because I thought it would be glamorous & luxurious, & which my mother consistently maintained would get filthy (being her house, it never did); wooden IKEA chest still almost overflowing with dressing-up clothes. Two half walls are filled with books from the early eras of my reading life — Enid Blyton & Maud Hart Lovelace & Diana Wynne-Jones & *Pongwiffy* & Tarka the Otter, three different versions of *Mrs Dalloway*, a full set of old Penguin Austens, Latin textbooks from my ill-fated foray into the School of Classics in my first year of university, *A Series of Unfortunate Events* stacked on top of each other to save space, their covers sunlight-faded.

Not that long ago the plan was to finally clear out this room & turn it into a bedroom & study for my father, no longer relegated to the attic for his snoring. I would move into his office, & all my things could be put in storage before, at long last, being moved to some mythical permanent residence of my own (in *this* economy, ha). It didn't transpire in time, but the desk being moved over to the window — where my bed had been since I was a teenager — was the remnant of such notions.

And sitting at it, do I feel nostalgic? Does a poignant but elegant little tear slip down my cheek, only to be bravely brushed away as I plough on with writing a draft chapter of my PhD that I am steadfastly working on because it is due to be with my supervisor in two days?

It does not. I am filled solely with rage & anxiety. I have not written a word of the chapter, though I have written hundreds of words of WhatsApp messages to my partner, who is staying with friends in Edinburgh & being treated like a king in a way that I cannot possibly compete with because to do so for a lifetime would be unsustainable. I think I must feel the way single parents feel when their ex takes the kids to Legoland for the weekend & lets them get sick from some colossal dessert piled high with whipped cream that maybe one of the kids is a little bit allergic to but they don't know that because they haven't been around to ferry said child to the doctor's. Of course, my wonderful, kind, good-egg friends have substituted Legoland & possible lactose intolerance for an abortion rally & homemade cinnamon rolls but the result is the same: I feel vengeful, uncharitable, & exhausted by my own inadequacy.

The most self-sustainingly frustrating thing about rage is that, being an irrational emotion (distinct, in this sense, from cold fury or self-righteous anger), it is so often completely unjustified. As I sit at the desk in Leeds, not writing my chapter, I am filled with two types of this unfair, uncalled-for, cruel rage. One is directed north, towards Edinburgh, my generous friends, & the love of my life — for essentially being good to one another & having a nice day. And one is directed downstairs, to my mother.

Up until my father died, I think I had seen her cry twice. Or at least this was the narrative I had built for myself — having told so many other people this in order to convey her strength, her pragmatism, & especially the contrast with my sentimental, soppy father, I no longer have any idea of its accuracy. However, on a shelf in my childhood bedroom is the terrible evidence of at least one occasion of maternal tears. It is a slight book called *River Boy* — a white cover with a blue figure like a Matisse cut-out. When I was about eight, I received it for Christmas. Sat on the rug we used to have on the floor of the living room, with its fat blue border & abstract green & orange shapes, its rough comfort, I unwrapped it & immediately announced to my mother that I had *told* her I didn't want this book when she'd pointed it out in Waterstone's a few weeks earlier. She left the room inconspicuously. When, on my father's insistence, I followed her upstairs, I found her sat on the edge of the bed, wiping her nose & trying to compose herself. It was, for point of comparison, the exact kind of secret crying that Emma Thompson does in *Love,*

Actually upon realising that Alan Rickman is almost certainly having an affair: necessary but perfunctory — the crying of a woman who does everything she can for her family & even after they have betrayed her, continues to hold it together for their sake. I find it difficult to watch that scene; the way she stuffs the tissue down her sleeve, pulls back her shoulders as she sniffs, smooths the already smooth bedspread — I feel it like tar on my organs.

Now, my mother cries. This is, of course, right. Only to be expected. Healthy, even. Her partner of almost thirty years, the father of her children, swiped from her with almost no notice. But every time her mouth tightens & her brow crumples, a selfish, horrific bile rises in me & it's all I can do to prevent it spilling over.

C.S. Lewis, *A Grief Observed*: 'I cannot talk to the children about her. The moment I try, there appears on their faces neither grief, nor love, nor fear, nor pity, but the most fatal of all non-conductors, embarrassment. They look as if I were committing an indecency. They are longing for me to stop. I felt just the same after my own mother's death when my father mentioned her. I can't blame them. It's the way boys are.'

Let's not go into the way boys are; it's the way children are. Bad children like me who can't handle their strong mothers' brief forays into weakness.

(It is at this point that either Moss or my therapist would raise their eyebrows and say *weakness?* Yes yes I know but I stand by it: this grief has made me weak & rage is my transcendence. Light it on fire & use it for something — wet wick made incandescent & at least that's *doing something*.)

On the anniversary of his death, people are reaching out. A tupperware box of almond brownies appears on our front step from the mother of an old school friend of mine, their family having always been close to mine. An email from my father's cricketing friend describes all the things he wishes he could tell my dad over a curry (between the poppadoms & actually ordering — my father took his time over this as in

74

all things): match scores & CLP gossip & Brexit Brexit Brexit.

(not for the first time, I consider the silver lining that the man who wore an EU lapel pin in all his suit jackets died before they actually triggered Article 50)

In *The Red Parts*, her account of the trial surrounding the murder of her aunt, Maggie Nelson writes about sitting in the courtroom and witnessing her mother's grief:

> My sister and I escaped to the bathroom at a break, and there Emily told me that she could barely look at our mother. She simply could not bear to see her in so much pain. I agreed, but did not confess to the less-admirable emotion. I also felt angry. I wanted our mother to meet these details with squared shoulders. I couldn't bear the way this man's words were shriveling her body into that of a little girl. I didn't want her to turn away; I didn't want her to shake.

When a parent dies (I think), it is not as if one piece of your family is missing. It is as if you get a whole new family. I didn't want a new one.

I sit at this desk that he should have sat at & never did. I sit & wish I had never seen my mother cry. I sit & wish for something other than what I have: instead of a father who cries & a mother who doesn't, I have a mother who cries, & a father who doesn't.

A woman on a podcast says: you do not have what you used to have, that is all grief is.

Seneca, exiled to Corsica, writes to his mother Helvia. It has been a while (& the exile thing was definitely his fault), so he's making excuses:

> I realised that your grief should not be intruded upon while it was fresh and agonising, in case the consolations themselves should rouse and inflame it: for an illness too nothing is more harmful than premature treatment.

She has lost her son because he fucked Caligula's sister. He tells her he's okay, he's okay. He tells her she should be too.

> So I was waiting until your grief of itself should lose its force and, being, softened by time to endure remedies, it would allow itself to be touched and handled.

I wonder if, despite herself, despite being lectured on her feelings by her own son, Helvia feels the way I do when I read this somewhere on the internet: that he is right. Grief as something not to be prematurely touched. Grief as too-hot-to-handle. I didn't even want to look at it.

He is right, again, later in the *consolatio*, when he makes his prescription:

> I am leading you to that resource which must be the refuge of all who are flying from Fortune, liberal studies [...] Return now to these studies and they will keep you safe. They will comfort you, they will delight you; and if they genuinely penetrate your mind, never again will grief enter there, or anxiety, or the distress caused by futile and pointless suffering. Your heart will have room for none of these, for to all other failings it has long been closed. Those studies are your most dependable protection, and they alone can snatch you from Fortune's grip.

[Reader, I went back to Edinburgh & my PhD pretty sharpish.]

The second time Moss came up from London (our "second date"), I suggested we go to the opening of an exhibition at a small gallery quite near my flat. This was an absolutely blatant attempt to present both myself & my city as cool, avant-garde, & whatever the opposite of parochial is. It was a members' show, wildly hit & miss, & so avant-garde as to almost circle back round to parochial again. The highlight, however, was a performance piece by a young woman who silenced the busy single-room gallery by wordlessly laying out a very large piece of paper on the floor & lying down on it. She then took a pair of scissors & began to cut around her own outline in little snips, her hand forced into awkward contortions. The process was agonisingly slow. As the room held its breath, Moss held my hand & I would occasionally shift my weight back into him so that our hips touched. Perhaps for this reason, this piece was, for me, about tension. The tension of the paper as the artist snagged her scissors on it, the tension of the room as we watched her snip so close to the soft skin between her fingers, the tension of Moss & I wanting each other, the current in the small space between us.

When we left, though, Moss said he thought it was about the boundaries of the self, about the ways in which the female or feminized body is made permeable. I was resistant to this reading in a way that surprised me. But I am learning that when I feel that immediate resistance to an idea, that snag that makes me dismissive & snappy, it is usually because the idea is true, & I do not want it to be. Because the thought of the feminized body — *my* body — as pervious, as unable to sustain its own outline, as consistently assumed to be available, penetrable (ugh, & there's the thing, isn't it? What we're talking about is violation, as usual. What a painful, dangerous, tedious snooze it is to be a woman) is distasteful to me.

Because it's not really about the body. It's about the self. If my body cannot be a boundaried thing, then my self becomes amorphous too. This is, of course, the whole bloody point & Moss was, as usual, right. But I began to wonder if such a reading would have irritated me *before* (everything now being *after*), if my self wouldn't have felt like such a slippery, unboundaried thing if I still had a father.

Judith Butler: 'It is not as if an "I" exists independently over here and then simply loses a "you" over there, especially if the attachment to "you" is part of what composes who "I" am. If I lose you, under these conditions, then I not only mourn the loss, but I become inscrutable to myself. Who "am" I, without you? When we lose some of these ties by which we are constituted, we do not know who we are or what to do. One one level, I think I have lost "you" only to discover that "I" have gone missing as well.'

You hold me in our 3/4 size double bed with the blind halfway up
because you like it dark & I like it light & I massage the scar tissue
on your chest & wonder if this is the idyllic queer domesticity I
always thought I might get to have.

In the early days, doing long-distance Edinburgh—London,
Moss & I spent endless hours on the phone. Sometimes
literally endless in that we would fall asleep together, our
headphones jammed in our ears as one of us drifted out of
consciousness & the other whispered *are you asleep* a couple of
times (a little hopeful, a little disappointed) before dissolving
into the dark too. Some mornings I'd wake up to find the call
still going, & tiny erosions on my cheek from the headphone
wire, as if he'd been there — & silently left.

Mostly during these calls I would walk, & often he would
be walking too, both of us making strange tracks around
our cities. I often fall into the habit of picturing these tracks
quite literally, envisioning some digital map where the
mundanities of my daily movements are recorded, a little
Rosa icon gliding through space, trailing an orange line
behind her. (Bizarrely, the person I usually imagine to be
checking these paths & making note of my step count is a
particular ex from university, whom my subconscious clearly
regards as continuing to sit in judgement of me.) This idea is,
I'm sure, the product of wild narcissism, but nevertheless it
arrives involuntarily on a regular basis.

In those days I would walk miles just to stay on the phone,
always taking the long route home, & doing weird loops
around my neighbourhood once I got too close to my
building. This was partly in order to avoid having to continue
the call inside, where my flatmate could overhear the tiny
intimacies of our quotidian chat, but also partly in order to
remain, essentially, nowhere. The feeling of being *between*,
of existing neither where I'd left, nor where I was arriving;
the liminality of the love-space, when no one knows where
you are.

[my other liminal space — that train journey: where the worst
is actually happening; the worst thing is going on as the train
moves & keeps moving & you're stuck not moving on this

79

moving thing & you need it to be faster because the worst
thing is happening *right now* & you're helpless but you need
it to be slower because the worst thing is happening in Leeds
& you're somewhere between Darlington & Doncaster & until
you're there it's *not happening* it's just *about to*]

Sometimes I feel like nothing that's happened since he died is real, or matters. Maybe that's an excuse for why I've stopped trying, but occasionally I can look at myself in the mirror — 27 years old, the first age he's never seen me at — & I spread my arms apart (on one of them is a tattoo he's never seen) & stare at this shitty Magdalen-Christ in a huge Les Mis t-shirt & look right through her. How do you understand yourself when half your home, half your DNA, half your childhood, half the people that have known you since the second you first sobbed at contact with this beautiful hellhole world simply does not exist any more? No wonder my reflection has scarpered.

Or when she is there, I hate her. Self-hatred, in my book, is the most perfect, the most pure form of hatred. & I truly believe it's very productive — I don't think anything motivates me better than a healthy dose of *you are a fucking useless piece of shit, change your life, change your fucking life*.

It *is* rage, by the way, that fuels Rilke in 'Archaic Torso of Apollo.' It is there in the 'ripening fruit' of the god's absent eyes, the hot chest 'suffused with brilliance from inside, / like a lamp.' It is there in 'that dark center where procreation flared,' and the way the stone 'glisten[s] like a wild beast's fur.' Rage is what makes the statue, 'from all the borders of itself, / burst like a star,' because *my god* 'You must change your life.'

[hot take sidenote: James Wright in 'Lying in a Hammock at William Duffy's Farm in Pine Island, Minnesota' is also full of rage. Don't be tricked by the idyll of ravines and cowbells and butterflies and pines. There is horse shit that 'Blaze[s] up' & a darkening sky & a hawk on the hunt. Do not underestimate the fury of 'I have wasted my life.' *I have wasted my life*.]

I've always been very good at this self-directed fury. & I've never felt hatred like the kind I've felt since I started looking at my reflection like this — as an alien thing. The lack of recognition gives me a blank glassiness that is then reflected back at me more; exponential growth, the reverse half-life of self-hatred.

I know this is all a bit much, a bit self-indulgent, & that if I just took a shower & maybe stopped listening to so many Springsteen songs that remind me he'll never get to see *Springsteen on Broadway* with me I'd probably feel a lot better.

Yes, but what is grief but melodrama?

I try to sing in the key between major & minor; the one that holds *this is certain & quotidian & the natural cycle of everything & boring selfish boring* at the same time as *yes but the world ended for someone & you loved him*

& it is sharp-flat dischord & will not be notated.

Halfway through 'Wherever You Are, Be Somewhere Else,' Denise Riley writes —

> I can try on these gothic riffs, they do make
> a black twitchy cloak to both ham up and so
> perversely dignify my usual fear of ends

& I think, what a thing for the melodramatic, the hammy, to be a dignifier of fear.

For Riley, the elaborate turn of phrase, the collapse into melodrama is a sartorial choice: the gothic riffs/ruffs, the vampy widow's cloak. We need such aesthetic choices in order to legitimise the embarrassment of how much we feel.

ham it up to make it real / ham it up to make it palatable

When you open the door you want people to see what they expect: drawn face, dark rings, mismatched clothing, the known trappings of loss. This is legible. This gives them permission to say that they are *sorry* (you are pitiable), they are *happy to do anything to help* (you are incapacitated), they are *here for you* (you are alone).

Do not open the door with a smile. Do not wave off their need to talk about it (they will not know how to talk about anything else). Do not say 'anyway, how are *you*?'

Gothic riffs: anything that they can say 'I know, I know' in response to.
Black twitchy cloak: anything that covers up everyone else's fear (of death, of faux pas, of you).

After her brother's death, Alice Notley began writing what she termed a "female" or "feminine" epic. Notley's brother had been a combatant in the Vietnam War, & then came home to a life of PTSD & addiction, & a death of the same. *The Descent of Alette* is a poem that emerged out of grief as frustration, grief as powerlessness. For Notley, the relationship between women & the epic is this — women (in this case Notley, her mother, her sister-in-law) 'were being used, mangled, by the forces which produce epic, and we had no say in the matter, never had, and worse had no story ourselves. We hadn't acted. We hadn't gone to war. [...] We got to suffer, but without a trajectory. We didn't even get to behave badly, or hurt anyone as a consequence (that would have been a story).'

[*Women are machines for suffering* says Picasso, & lets their suffering move into an abstract *always already*, away from cause, away from blame, away from him.]

Grief is something that happens to women. Over & over, 'through the whole long universe' (says Alice).

It happens to me over & over. The bouncing ball, the button pushed.

I think of Greek laments as a "female" art form.
I think of my father's cousin, Patricia, singing another Irish lament at another funeral.
(I think of Pothos [Greek: Πόθος "yearning"]*)*

POTHOS, brother of EROS and HIMEROS, winged love-god. POTHOS, son of APHRODITE? [maybe] / son of ZEPHYROS & IRIS [maybe].

PLATO says *the name* himeros *(longing) was given to the stream* (rhous) *which most draws the soul; for because it flows with a rush* (hiemenos) *and with a desire for things and thus draws the soul on through the impulse of its flowing, all this power gives it the name of* himeros. *And the word* pothos *(yearning) signifies that it pertains not to that which is present, but to that which is elsewhere* (allothi pou) *or absent, and therefore the same feeling which is called* himeros *when its object is present, is called* pothos *when it is absent.*

POTHOS as unrequited love, love in absence, love with nowhere to go, with stilled wings.

POTHOS in Nonnus' *Dionysiaca*: The unwarlike gods of love, fighting for King Minos: 'I know how tender Pothos sacked a city,' he writes.

Orange POTHOS in the air at the Getty, sprinkling nectar.

Precise POTHOS on a vase at the British Museum, he & his brothers looking remarkably like John & George & Ringo (no Paul). EROS carries a hare, HIMEROS a sash, POTHOS a wreath that wanders, vinelike, all curls and scrolls.

Elsewhere—

THEOPHRASTUS
HISTORIA PLANTARUM
(*Enquiry into Plants*)
(*and minor works on odours and weather signs*)
(in two volumes)
trans. Sir Arthur Hort (1916)

'[...] also the plant called 'regret,' of which there are two kinds, one with a flower like that of a larkspur, the other not coloured but white, which is used at funerals; and this one lasts longer.'

'[*cf.* the Eng. plant-name 'love-in-absence'; see πόθος in Index]'

πόθος: pothos

For the Ancient Greeks, celery & parsley were funereal flowers.

I found that out from Wikipedia in order to write a poem.

I wish I could say that every time I eat them I think of my dad but I definitely don't.

I wish I could say that the poem was good but it keeps losing poetry competitions.

I wish I could say that I performed small interesting rituals with celery & parsley in the early days of my grief. I wish I could describe them for you here so that you would find me complex & idiosyncratic.

I wish that grief made me complex & idiosyncratic but the more I think about it the more profoundly basic it seems.

Last year I saw someone with the fact of their bereavement in their Twitter bio & I almost went blind with rage. I saw some version of myself in the cyberdark void & the void looked back & thought it made them special & *choking* on fury   I saw that neither of us were.

Moments of biblical mourning: Jesus goes to his death (a certain train, a fast train through Jerusalem), & a crowd follows him in the streets *of women, which also bewailed and lamented him*. He turns on them: *Daughters of Jerusalem, weep not for me, but weep for yourselves, and for your children* [...] *For if they do these things in a green tree, what shall be done in the dry?* Translation: worse things happen at sea.

Women follow him in the streets, women attend the crucifixion, go to his grave, weep weep weep endlessly. Mary is as lachrymose as they come, & now there's a miraculous weeping Madonna wherever you might care to find her.

Modern psychology (apparently) holds that there are two kinds of grief: instrumental & intuitive. Instrumental grievers will keep busy, compartmentalise, take on new responsibilities, avoid expressions of emotion, possibly make jokes about dead dads two weeks later that will make their friends glance at each other & shift uncomfortably in their seats.

Intuitive grievers rely on others, explore their feelings, express them outwardly & sincerely — they "process."

I should not need to add that every internet article I've read about these kinds of grief makes them gendered. *Women*, as if that were any kind of stable or coherent category, are more likely to lean intuitive, & thus women's grief is, on average (as it were), considered the more "appropriate" kind. Double-down on this with western patriarchy's discomfort with emotional men & the cycle repeats. Women telling the story of their grief over & over 'through the whole long universe.' Processing over & over, turning it over & over. New lamentations, repeated lamentations. New tears on the statues of Mary — oil, blood, honey. All our grief made manifest in the figure of the weeping woman: Niobe, Antigone, Giotto's *The Lamentation*, Dora Maar biting her nails for Picasso, Jackie Kennedy, Chris Ofili's *No Woman No Cry*, Esaw Garner, *Mater Dolorosa, pietà pietà pietà*.

> *Thus says the Lord of hosts, 'Consider and call for the mourning women, that they may come; And send for the wailing women, that*

they may come! Let them make haste and take up a wailing for us,
that our eyes may shed tears and our eyelids flow with water.'

Always in the back of my mind: *the plants need watering, the plants need watering.*

At first, I was good at it. Green-thumbed & nonchalant, things just sort of sprouted up around the flat. Endless new leaves on the pothos, the ivy trailing picturesquely off the side of the mantelpiece, the supermarket basil becoming lush & abundant, the schefflera pushing out sprig after sprig. I bought my soil from Poundland, planted seeds at arbitrary times of the year, didn't use drainage systems or a mister, had no idea which way was South. Still, things grow.

Somewhere in the Yorkshire Dales, Moss & I cross a cattle-grid carpeted in soft grasses & I tell him how, as a kid, I liked to picture myself as some sort of sprite or minor god, leaving such greenery as a kind of snail trail, materialising behind me. Later, he finds the image in a description of Aphrodite: *where she steps, flowers bloom*. I think: nice.

But as soon as I become aware of what I'm doing (love — love in another place — channeled into growth), it's like a curse has been cast. I try too hard, I overwater, I plant too many tomato seeds in the same pot & they all sprout shoots, their roots too enmeshed to separate. They become ungainly, monstrously tall, crowding the kitchen window, blocking out the light. The tendrils of the miniature cucumbers squeeze the life out of the pepper plants, the parsley can't find a patch of sun. One of the ivys gets moved into the bedroom & is never seen again, dying a dry death on top of the wardrobe. The miniature cactus from E that has guarded my desk for years (a minor talisman of love less-spoken, of something spiky & enduring) gets put outside the door of the flat in a fit of pride, & someone nicks it.

My friend Rosie is the true cattle-grid Aphrodite. Next to the grow-light & the humidifier she paints her plants into being with tiny brushstrokes: grey, green, add the white, the ochre, thick on the delicate brush. *Monstera albo*, high-sheen gloss like bathroom lacquer, bleached clean, produces its other into spontaneous page-space. *Hoya linearis* scatters forth, with thick little leaves just begging to be crushed. The *maranta leuconeura* is too unreal to be painted, but there are watercolour ferns, their botanical elements neatly excised, labelled at the bottom of the page. *Syngonium* mottled sits as a single leaf in blank space, its parent hovering over the canvas, wondering how it shedded so cleanly, & without noticing.

Her garden *grows*, baby.

Three days before my thirtieth birthday, Moss smuggles a large flat package into the box room. Squared away inside is a satin pothos, sprung forth from Rosie's painterly hand, a propogation, of a kind, but ever-living. We plant it on the wall above the white shelves of novels, where it nestles behind the dracaena, real/unreal & perfect.

Plants know how to bend, know how to push against the edges of things, to lean always to the light. Rooted in circumstance, they alter & are altered in turn.

Curve of the tomato plant stems, hitting the window frame // delicate spiraling tendrils of cucumber vine, clinging to the window-blind cords as if they've had enough sun (*tug tug*) // after being subject to multiple propagation cuttings, one of the pothos vines takes off in an entirely new direction // inch-by-inch rotations of the monstera, whose wide flat leaves are slowly giving way to new growth: artfully fenestrated, finally.

Round the corner live Dianne & Kate, whose colossal monstera seems to emerge from the very bowels of the house, peering ominously over the landing into the hallway to greet guests. I have no sense of it having a pot, rather that both house and plant grew at the same time, out of necessity.

Recently I've had this single sentence repeating in my head like an involuntary mantra —

Frida Kahlo painted masterpieces whilst lying on her back in unimaginable pain.

Somehow the exact phrasing of it matters — it's not the knowledge of Kahlo's almost mythological fortitude that I'm invoking, but something in the banality of the invocation. It feels remembered, rather than conjured; familiar enough to be a quotation, prosaic enough to be from anywhere. I have a slight suspicion it might be from a *Babysitters' Club* book, which is one of the reasons I haven't googled it.

Frida Kahlo painted masterpieces whilst lying on her back in unimaginable pain.

It is, more than anything, an admonishment. It says, *do something.* It says, *make something out of this.* It says, *don't be pathetic.*

I feel pathetic. I feel barely able to rise from any given seat, I feel hazy from the codeine, I feel snuffling & weak like some kind of little animal. Except I don't feel little, I feel like a sprawling mass of flesh that can't leverage itself off the soft furnishings properly. I feel like the open wound on my inner thigh *is* me: vulnerable & disgusting & difficult to look at directly. Something to be worried about, but never loved. Something deeply, deeply undesirable. Not like Frida —

Frida Kahlo painted masterpieces whilst lying on her back in unimaginable pain.

Frida, goddess of strength & vigilance, not trapped in her body but using it, wiry & electric & burning.

I eye the fairy cakes Moss made last night out of his anxiety & then under the table at the body that has let me down.

I can feel myself just one associative sentence away from thinking stupid thoughts like *maybe if I was thin I would wear the pain better. Maybe I would look wan & strained & hollow-cheeked & then I could be the kind of stoic invalid that people admire.*

One of my favourite books as a child was *What Katy Did* by Susan Coolidge. Katy was this brash, headstrong scruffbag of a kid with a big imagination, a good heart, & a short temper (so far, so *Anne of Green Gables*, my other favourite). Defying the commands of some authority figure or other, she falls from a broken swing & is forced to spend years immobile, cut off from anything outside the four walls of her sick room, trapped by her pain. Katy's mentor is the angelic invalid Cousin Helen, who counsels her to treat pain as a teacher, strict but loving. Imbued with this philosophy, Katy is transformed from a Bad Invalid to a Good Invalid; from impatient & complaining — all sweat & anger & unbrushed hair in a dingy, foetid room — to a patient patient, able to serenely manage her little household through love & a humble acceptance of her fate.

& for her efforts she is seemingly rewarded by a miraculous — albeit slow — recovery. (Cousin Helen does not recover, true angels never do.)

The struggles of my plants are never beautiful. The crash of porcelain on porcelain as the wind tunnel down the hall between two open windows causes yet another seedling to be flung from the sill into the toilet bowl is not beautiful. It is annoying & I find myself on the floor scooping teaspoons of soil from the linoleum because I'm too lazy to buy a new bag of compost. When the cucumber tendrils strangle their own leaves or the courgette puts out another yellow dud I don't think *I admire how quiet & strong you are, how little you complain*.

I get out the kitchen scissors. I have no time for their poor attempts. I snip out the offending item & I tell them to get on with it. Their little wounds heal, & they are stronger because they've stopped putting precious energy into trying to keep alive something that was not serving them well.

(I don't know what I'm supposed to learn from this.)

Frida Kahlo painted masterpieces whilst lying on her back in unimaginable pain.

I don't know much about unimaginable pain. The cyst & the surgery & the open wound & all that hurt a lot, but it's long-since healed. Once you're outside it, pain feels impossible to remember. I suppose that's why people keep having babies.

Grief (ah yes, here we go)—
Grief is unimaginable. As in, I don't know what it feels like. I don't know if I've done it or had it or felt it. I don't know if it's painful. I know that occasionally I will think about how I don't have a father any more when I thought I would have one for ages & I will end up on the floor of the corridor & Moss will have obscene amounts of snot matted into in his chest hair & it will feel like I could not possibly ever stop crying. That seems both painful & unimaginable. I can't remember how that feels. That was yesterday.

Frida Kahlo painted masterpieces whilst lying on her back in unimaginable pain.

The propagated pothos just put out one warped, twisted little leaf. A masterpiece.

The thing about pain is it makes you selfish. You fold in yourself, unable to see beyond the boundaries of your own useless body. You can't understand why everyone else doesn't *get it*, doesn't feel your pain, isn't asking you about it constantly, why it isn't the centre of their world as it is yours.

(*no one has asked me about the death of my father in many months*)

At present, the centre of my world is an open wound located delightfully in the crease between my left inner thigh & my vulva; the result of surgery to remove something even more repulsive. I can't sleep, I can't walk. I want to do both of those things quite a lot.

I stare at the Christmas cactus in the little ceramic hanger on the wall. That is, I'm assuming it's a Christmas cactus, but it hasn't yet flowered & it's February. In fact, it hasn't flowered in the three years I've lived here — one of Jen's, left behind because it was dark & shriveled & static. After Sean moved out & Moss moved in I *dealt with* all the plants, suddenly houseproud & very interested in this little space that we had fought so hard for. Being in love means you stay in a lot. It means you wander about your home, gazing at it — the scenery, the backdrop, the props of your love — with a kind of hazy scrutiny. Suddenly a two-leaved monstera was not acceptable, a crap English ivy, a yellowing pothos. Suddenly a dry little cactus was simply not pulling its weight. I repotted, pruned, propagated, & snuck bits of greenery into IKEA trolleys. The cactus loved its new spot in the bedroom overlooking our sex life, snuggling down into the new soil & putting out glossy segments of stem, each chunk heralded by a furry tip at the end of the previous one. There is a slight fashionable pinkness to its edges.

This, I think bitterly, *is all I have to offer*.

I am trying to learn to grow up. To allow my life to become a little smaller so that it can grow vast inside me. To focus in on my home, this family I am trying to make, these spaces inside spaces (desk in living room, womb in body, bubble of air in soup on stove). I am learning to tend my garden; talking to my houseplants, less afraid to touch their baby leaves, to feed them water from my own cup, to occasionally dig my hands into their root systems & unpick & snip & tug. They are responding.

What I'm saying is that I'm trying to throw smaller parties. Trying to look a Friday night dead in the eye & put on fluffy socks. Trying to remind myself that I do not think less of people who work hard, who love their partners, who keep a tidy house — that I do not believe that a quote unquote *exciting life* makes for exciting work, & that anyway we need to reframe the *exciting*, the *interesting*, the *vast*. There is such space in this home.

It's almost too obvious & gauche to even say, but Plath's best work came from a life grown almost unbearably small. Woolf never travelled, yet her letters to Vita are as full & spacious as the ones Vita sent from abroad. Dickinson — well, it really doesn't need to be said.

I think of Amy Key and Rebecca Perry secreted away at Halsway Manor, living small witchy lives together among the knotted trees & the high ceilings. I think of Nat Raha, further down in Leith, considering the whale harpoon. I think of Sophie Robinson, alone on the beach at Fire Island, with her back to the waves. I think of Zein, near-far in her bedroom in Amman. I think of Becky 'in America getting coffee all over myself & smiling a lot & pressing buttons on my aircon unit at random & walking around my empty apartment & opening then closing the same 3 word documents & consistently getting to the grocery shop too late to buy a $7 punnet of cherry tomatoes.' I think of Alexa, two streets away, making tea with Charlotte Salomon, before putting her down to crush Justin in their endless Jeopardy competition. It is okay to put down a book & pick up your partner's hand. (It is okay to hold both & nothing else.) It is okay to leave a room full of people who do not love you & go home to houseplants that

do. It is okay to be loved only by four people if you love those four people with your whole heart.
I am learning.

It is not a lot to learn, & perhaps I should have learned it much earlier, much faster, & with rather less help from houseplants, but here we are: little shoots are pushing up on the windowsill, the monstera has four fat leaves, the seeds from Rosie's wedding have become thick curlicues of something that looks like salad greens, the basil is flowering delicately at the top of its wavering twiglet stems, there are nine perfect leaves on each protrusion from the schefflera, & I —

& I & I & I

— am okay. Am a sprouting thing. Am trying.

Grief: A Methodology—

1. It refuses.

1. One vignette at a time.
2. Alexa, consummate Virgo, upon being asked how things are, says that she's so busy and exhausted she barely has time to grieve. I, consummate Sagittarius, sagely remind her that grief doesn't work like that, that it cannot be scheduled in.
3. It's not even a *thing*.
4. (I am a liar, because I have repeatedly scheduled it *out*.)
5. The sea.
6. Chloë goes to the sea every day. I don't know whether she always thinks about her brother.
7. Chloë walks into the sea, holding a huge ream of bubble wrap that threatens to overwhelm her, sturdy as she is in her black shift. It begins to unravel, to be whipped by the wind.
8. Chloë gathers it in, but with each new grasp comes a new release, and the bubble wrap becomes more unwieldy than ever. It is stressful to watch.
9. Chloë walks through a haar-filled twilight, still juggling her bundle.
10. I pause the video, put my eyeball very close to the screen. Maybe it's not even bubble wrap.

Grief: A Timeline?

18 September 2017
Holly: d'you want me 2 ask how ur doing or nah
Me: not sure honestly
Me: nah probs not I guess, doesn't feel the time

20 September 2017
Holly: how was the appt yesterday?
Me: sort of good, in that he is eligible for for chemo, but sort of less good in that there's about a 50% chance of it taking, which means a 50% chance of a timescale of years rather than months (which my mam seemed pretty pleased about, but I didn't know yet that that was what we were looking at so it was like: shock! but also maybe good news!)

29 September 2017
15:49
Holly: friend are you ok?
Me: don't worry — could you call me after your meeting?
Me: no worries at all if not

19:33
Holly: hey friend. hope you're okay and got there safe — would love to hear an update when you feel up to it but no pressure at all. call me any time. lots of love to you and your fam xxxxxxxx

21:16
Holly: i love you i love you i love you

In the Wellcome Collection, on a dark wood wall crowded with gold frames, somewhere to the right of the *Garden of earthly delights* (after Bosch)—

(see the lovers encased in a translucent bubble, seemingly organic as it emerges from a flesh-pink fruit out of which a man's face peers, expressionless; see the badger-bear perched on top of a hollow reddish fish, out of which poke a row of arses & legs, pert & perhaps joyful about being swallowed; see the man wearing an upturned flower on his head as he humps a tomato giant enough to be mistaken for an exercise ball)

—& low to the ground is a small ex-voto oil painting. In it, a woman cowers by the bed, her left arm outstretched to deflect an attacker who lunges toward her with a stiletto knife in his hand. A small child in sunny yellow stretches their chubby limbs toward the woman's neck, looking for sanctuary — she holds them but her face is turned away, to the top left of the frame where a tiny Madonna is suspended in the empty space before the wall, emitting light.

The woman appeals across the bed, the man wears a brown suit.

The very fact this painting exists to hang in a museum on Euston Road, below & to the right of a large & not very famous not-quite-Bosch, means that this scene is not a scene, but a memory. It means that this woman survived. That the Madonna intervened & stayed the man's hand — or gave this woman the means to do so herself. Her blue dress — not very brilliant, not very beautiful — somehow holds all the power of this possibility, this thanks. The hard times pass. You get through. You make something.

The last of the tomato plants was germinated late in the season, the only survivor out of an egg-box of six. Crowded out of the coveted sunny kitchen window by its already-huge cousins, it perched instead on the bathroom sill, stunted further, no doubt, by the frosted glass. Everything in our flat comes off a long corridor that runs from our bedroom in the North-East to the bathroom in the South-West (which makes the flat sound pleasingly vast, as if you could find the West Midlands somewhere near the door to the box room), & when all the doors & windows are open — as they often are — a draught whips through, causing various unidentified crashes to sound throughout our home. Upon investigation, these are almost always plants that have leapt from their spots & deposited themselves & their soil in some kind of artistic pattern on the carpet. Bonus points if the pots or, worse, glass propagation jars, have got involved with the project of deconstruction.

Without fail, these incidents occur in the midst of existing human crisis. Smoke alarm goes off because I've had some kind of minor breakdown over breakfast & left the grill on? Throw all the windows open, plants fling themselves to the floor. Trying to clean the entire flat in two hours because my mother is visiting & I've left everything to the last minute because I let the entire day go by eating cheese on toast & watching increasingly poor quality videos of gender-swapped Broadway numbers? Better air the place by opening the windows! *Crash*, French beans & terracotta getting acquainted with the carpet right next to the sofa bed. Having an argument? No need to even have the windows open, all the hot air & rising temperatures & slamming doors will simply drive an aloe over the edge of the bookcase.

The last of the tomato plants threw himself off the bathroom ledge multiple times: once he shattered the chipped teacup he inhabited, once he lost all his soil just as my big bag of compost from Poundland had run out, once he dived directly into the toilet bowl. I moved him to our bedroom window, told him to stay still. He liked it there, grew tall & ungainly & in need of repotting—

—but it's nearly August in the present tense & I'm exhausted.

The compost bag is still empty, I've let the tomatoes & courgettes & miniature cucumbers obscure the kitchen window completely. There are four beautiful French beans on the [vines? bush?] on top of the filing cabinet that I have been fingering without picking for weeks. The aloe pup in the bathroom is going brown at the ends, none of my pothos cuttings are growing roots.

This morning, after a conversation with Moss (him in the shower, me with a cup of coffee leaning on the doorframe, him suggesting gently that it would be possible — perhaps even easy — to view the last few months of my PhD & my approach to work a bit differently, me suggesting — not so gently, & already choking on the words a bit — that this was a completely impossible idea, that I am a useless asshole with no work ethic & *I don't have time to overhaul my entire thinking so that I can somehow establish a routine I should have established three years ago, okay?*), I sat down on the bed & looked out of the window, flung wide on the hottest day of the year, & sobbed breathlessly because of the desperate A4 to-do list on the kitchen table & the overflowing laundry basket & the five unanswered texts & the (exciting! thrilling! wildly positive!) opportunity email languishing in my inbox with one of those gmail nudges (*received 14 days ago — reply?*), & Boris Johnson having just appointed his cabinet but I couldn't bear to look because I'm a coward & self-involved & the fact the weather was so beautiful & I wanted to be out in the sun getting a freckly tan because even if I was doomed to be the fat one who picked the wrong dress at my friend's wedding then damnit, I could at least have the kind of healthy glow that makes people say "you're looking well!" even when you're not Hot or Pretty & the fact that when I cry my stupid eyes get so puffy & the next day I always have a headache like a crying hangover like I've managed to excrete so much liquid that I'm actually hungover like the world won't let you cry without it ruining the next day too without reminding you that you're sad you're sad you're so fucking sad all the time you useless piece of shit.

This went on for six or seven minutes until the last of the tomato plants fell off the windowsill. His soft little top-fronds & his tiny yellow flowers reached across the books on my bedside table to my pillow. I righted him, scooped up the bits of loose soil, brushed my hands into his too-small pot, & got out of bed.

Since I started growing tomatoes I feel like they have taken on grand symbolic significance when I see them out in the world. The glistening bruschetta in the pub, the plastic bag of fat Moneymakers that the old guy in the striped t-shirt sets down on the end of our pub table next to his abstemious schooner, the beautiful range of heritages that my friend's partner produced from class-inflected brown paper this weekend, holding up huge scarlet ridged ones, sweet sunshine-yellow cherries, pale egg-shaped greens, fat ones speckled with aubergine purple, as we exclaimed over them in turn. A tomato salad now seems to me the most luxurious of offerings for guests — somehow seems to make manifest the kind of life I'm trying to make: beautiful, moderate, blessedly simple, covered in fancy salt flakes & good olive oil.

Moss has been in semi-serious prepper mode for months. There are nine tins of anchovies in the cupboard, eight of cannellini beans, sixteen of chopped tomatoes (it may be redundant to mention at this point, but yes, he is Italian). He bought a camping stove that uses twigs to not only heat food & water but also charge electronic devices. We buy loo roll in colossal bulk.

Sometimes, it is not funny. There are 7000 kinds of medication currently being stockpiled by the government as a no-deal contingency plan. I have no idea whether testosterone is one of them, but I highly doubt it. And if it is, it's reserved for cis men. Moss has started thinking about whether he should start requesting repeat prescriptions a little earlier than he needs, in case there are delays or shortages (or worse or worse or worse we don't know). I push back when he imagines chaos, talk about *being realistic*, about *Tory self-interest*, about *provisions*, but I'm scared. We're all scared.

Sometimes, we can make it funny. Moss walks into the living-room & requests that I do not kiss him for the next hour because he has just put hair-growth stuff on his moustache. *If Brexit means I might run out of testosterone, I want a full moustache before October*. We dub it his prepper 'stache.

107

I look at my five miniature cucumbers & two pairs of French beans & tiny crop of green tomatoes & one bold pepper & think: *ah*.

This is how it is: there is peace, then not. There is chaos, then not.

There is a bunch of daffodils on the warm wood table & a pothos curling in the background & perfect late afternoon sunlight, & then there is horror & gasping for air & a slick grey heat that lives in your blood.

There is a list that never ends & care digging into the space between your eyebrows & there is pain & pain & pain & pain & keeping going & never stopping, & then there is warm wet red dark relief, slipped into like a sleeping pill or an expensive pod for floating in.

Crying is, I suppose, a big part of it.

It wasn't for a long time: the gulping down, staring at myself in the mirror, forcing it back down, deep sniffs of air, slow down the breath, look yourself in the fucking eye stop stop stop.

Now—

Moss working a late-night shift, my legs almost unable to bend thanks to a spontaneous weightlifting session two days ago. Moss says that using new muscles causes tiny little tears in them, & that the pain is them repairing themselves. Coming back, harder better faster stronger. It makes me want to tear my skin off if I think about it. So: salts in the bath, hot water staining my thighs a hot bright pink, trying not to listen to Lana del Ray — god she loves to cry, loves to catalyse the tear ducts — focus on the book, focus. & then Springsteen. It's the new album, the one he's never heard, I can't hear him singing it, it's safe it's okay put the book down.

Sit up, look down the fairy-lit corridor for him. Cross your legs like you're a child again, so that the ghost can visit, can see your life, this beautiful beautiful life you built for yourself in the flat he only ever saw on the day you moved in. Why did he never come visit? This is the biggest regret, never making space in your beautiful adult life for your parents. Always too busy for them, never asking them in, never letting them stay for longer than was absolutely necessary.

The ghost comes down the corridor & you sob sob sob into your hands, steam & sweat & a throbbing head. You're naked but it doesn't matter because you're a child & your daddy is going to come in & wrap a huge soft towel around you & hold you until you stop convulsing with sobs, until the snot is wiped from your face, until Bruce stops singing, until his baby's come in on the Tucson Train. The ghost looks around, sees the yellow chairs in the kitchen, the bouquet leftover from your ex's wedding on the table, thinks it's so nice that you're still friends, he always liked him but is happier now you're happier, is always happy for you, is so proud. The artificial garlands strung through the fairy lights catch him on his balding head & he laughs & you turn your head up to the ceiling & clasp your wet hands full of snot & do what? Pray? Wish?

Weep. Weep weep weep until the water turns tepid. Wipe your face one last time. Get out. Wrap yourself in your own towel.

You may not begin again. You're already staring down the barrel of having to put the cold backs of spoons on your eyes tomorrow morning, no sense in making it worse, no sense in summoning up all that energy again — the heaving chest, the gasping for air — no sense in having to wash your clean face again. It doesn't help anyway. It never helps.

The tiny tears in my leg muscles make themselves known to me as I heave my gross wet floppy mass of an adult body out of the bath. They still hurt. Less though, now.

Not even mid September & already the spiders are coming in. Big brown things in the bathtub like a horrible morning alarm. Already people are posting pictures of mist & orange leaves on instagram, already Nigel Slater is recommending the comforts of rice pudding with syrupy plums. Already I am losing the will to give a shit.

The unpicked tomatoes are literally rotting in their clusters & the miniature cucumbers have turned a sour, nauseous shade of yellow, the vines suddenly disinterested in whatever loose wet sunlight deigns to come through the kitchen window. I have stopped watering them all, but haven't yet summoned the energy to get out a big black bag. Can you re-use the soil? Or is it infested with stringy root systems, rotting blackly & ruining a new seed's chances? Suddenly everything seems much less hopeful, much less productive. The pothos cuttings don't seem to be rooting, there's just green mulch at the bottom of every jar & shot glass. Once all the tomato plants are cleared from the kitchen window we'll finally have our view of the allotments back — but what shite timing, just as the frosts return & everyone brings in their garden furniture.

We made jam again this year, but it was a grey day & the strawberries weren't on as good a deal. Both stressed & distracted, we treated it as a task rather than a pleasure, slotted in between work & choir rehearsal. I took no pictures, wrote no poems. We didn't have sex.

We invite Alexa & Justin over, have a fight right before they arrive. Everyone cries that afternoon. Everyone is falling apart. We are holding each other together but there is still soil behind the toilet from the last un-dealt-with disaster. I make a vat of couscous & we drink sour beers. Alexa's father is dying in Canada & we cannot help. I have nothing to offer, her grief so layered with trauma, mine reduced to snot in the greying bathwater. We talk in turns for hours until Moss makes emergency late-night chicken & everyone shifts on the hard kitchen chairs. The next morning I walk into the living room & think about how we should have retired to the sofas, been surrounded by plants that *aren't* dying. The pothos bristles from its top shelf. The longest vine almost touches the floor now.

I read about Alexander Chee & his Brooklyn rose garden. The design, the precision, the palette, the Latin the Latin the Latin.

I tried it for a while:

calathea ornata

schefflera arboricola

kalanchoe pinnata

hedera helix

A litany may be a comfort

(Moss tells me about Italian masses in which saints are named endlessly while the congregation replies *prega per noi* over & over)

but it is not

of any practical use.

The *calathea ornata* ("the one you got for my birthday after thinking that the Kew Gardens shop was actually at the Edinburgh Botanic Gardens & being confused when you got there") is in direct sunlight & a pot too small & its purple undersides are turning brown at the edges.

The *schefflera arboricola* ("tree thing in the kitchen") keeps getting more ungainly, dropping its eight-leaf branch-things as it goes.

The *kalanchoe pinnata* ("leggy succulent thing with the waxy leaves") has been propagated so many times that I can't remember which was the original, but it used to sit on top of the cistern, leering.

The *hedera helix* is just ivy. I don't know what it needs.

Brexit, Coronavirus, crisis after crisis. We prep, stockpile a little. I go away for a few days in early March & receive an email from our joint Amazon account: *Your order of "Water Purification Tablets" and "Medieval Tapestries Colouring Book" will arrive in 3 days.* I am stood on the picket line with my colleagues & tell them. I wonder if my life is actually made up entirely of anecdotes & punchlines & vignettes or whether I have devised it that way myself. I think about buying more soil & do not.

In the early days of the pandemic, when death was still considered news, Moss tells me about a young man in Manchester who couldn't say goodbye to his father because the family had to self-isolate. He, Moss, cries & looks at me & I look at the blue of his eyes getting darker & at the way his forehead becomes a *brow* & at the slightly sarcastic comments I've written on the student essay I'm marking & wonder if I am a Very Bad Person.

It used to be that when I got caught up in so-called political "debates" with people, I would burst into tears within minutes. Shouting, sobbing, furious — *hysterical*. Now I've been poisoned with rhetoric about *bandwidth* & *capacity* & how little I have to spare of either. I disengage, draw a line somewhere between head & heart, tongue & throat, squeeze of vocal cords & tearducts, like the *you're dead* gesture, hand slicing over clavicle. Cut it off.

I mean this as a shrug, but nothing really ever was okay again after death came into my life properly. So now I think (*impassively*, *dispassionately*): how is the world going on? Almost everyone with that bit of death inside them. Huh.

I ask my students for their favourite part of 'The Waste Land' & a chorus of voices say *I did not know death had undone so many*.

When things are very hard & Moss is very ill & our little flat is barely holding itself together, Bella texts me *I hope your plants are growing well* & it is like a blessing has settled over everything. Dust motes are stilled by early evening sunlight, the fruit bowl glows with juice. The washing machine hits the part of the cycle that's like a breath being released, I crack my spine.

Working hard is hard work but the plants don't show it. When they're growing well I don't need to do anything. I can spend a whole day in a frozen state of panic, or soporific torpor, & the plants will still grow.

The plants forgive me, I think.

In *Grief is the Thing with Feathers*, Ted Hughes' foetid, filthy Crow becomes the bereavement nurse for a grieving family, because why not. In the voice of his Boys, growing up without their mother, Max Porter writes, devastatingly, 'We hope she likes us.'

This is the thing no one can offer me. No amount of *he was so proud, he loved you so much* can be the rug that covers the curling lino of *he does not know me any more*.

Three years of becoming, three years growing— what? drier than ever? fat new leaves? a different colour of flower to the ones he relied on to bloom each spring?

Sausage fat black on the spatula as my mother moves the geraniums inside for the winter, fifteenth year in a row, but first (so obvious it's unsayable, unthinkable) without him.

My mother can't fill the dishwasher sufficiently any more. The fridge is too big. She still makes Christmas cake but I have no idea who is eating it because only my father ever did.

When Moss & I move in with her for two months because he is sick/recovering & I am finishing my PhD & we are Not Coping—

[*the washing up is endless, the laundry never seems to dip below the top of the basket no matter how many loads I do, I make pasta e fagioli every night, each time more hastily, not peeling the carrots, my soffrito less & less finely diced, I fill the hot water bottle eight times a day, we cry every night*]

—my mother comments repeatedly on how much we eat. I realise with something akin to shock that she has spent almost three years shopping & cooking for one.

Each year the geraniums move back & forth, outliving him.

In Don Paterson's 'Funeral Prayer,' he writes of death as apotheosis, as culmination. We gather at the end of a life, the poem says, 'because our friend is now complete.' It's a good thought, perhaps a helpful one. Someone whole & finished can be considered properly, after all, unlike the messy awfulness of trying to comprehend the shifting, confounding transience of a living personality.

But then there's Frank, who titles his elegy for Bunny Lang, 'The Unfinished' — a reflection of her mercilessly short life, her thwarted ambition, her relentless forward motion brought to a shuddering halt. Here, death is not completion, but a robbery. The poem wavers, constantly asserting & denying its own affect. In the first stanza, happiness 'goes off to cocktails without telling me why,' & so Frank declares:

> I will be as unhappy as I damn well
> please and not make too much of it because I am
> really here and not in a novel or anything or a jet plane

Later, he catches himself making too much of it: 'I'm impersonating some wretch weeping over a 1956 date book and of course / I pull myself together.'

The self-conscious theatricality of this is perhaps an imitation of Bunny, an actress who hammed up her whole life, whose own poetry is so affected & baroque as to be off-putting (& yet — marvellous). *Starring Frank O'Hara as: Bereaved!*

Joe LeSeueur, Frank's sometime lover & roommate, in *Digressions on Some Poems by Frank O'Hara* (a book that belongs alongside Woolf's *Orlando* as one of the greatest love letters in literature), writes that Frank carried his unfinished mourning with him all his life. 'I am not exaggerating about his grief,' he writes, recounting a time when someone, 'curious about Bunny, asked Frank what she was like. The mention of her name caught him off-guard; cut to the quick, he burst into tears and fled to his bedroom, as though he'd just received word of her death.'

I always thought plants had an apotheosis; that they reached a perfect lush stage & then just stuck there, huge & beautiful forever. At first this was all I was interested in: finished product, stasis. I wanted to simply summon a massive yucca from nothing. I wanted to just *be* the person I wanted to be, not to have to *become* it. I didn't want to have to start small.

We visit Moss' Great Aunt Sallie in her house in Helensburgh, a beautiful place full of blue glass & colour-coded doors & an ancient rocking horse that I am allowed to sit gingerly on. In one room is largest monstera I have ever seen. It towers over everything on its colossal moss pole, a jungle entity in its own personal Scottish hothouse. The fenestration is astonishing. I ask Sallie how long she's had it, & she says 'oh, twenty, thirty years' & I realise that not only does it hold within it years & years of becoming, but that it will keep going, under Sallie's uncareful eye. (I think I want to be Sallie when I grow up.)

Don finishes 'Funeral Prayer' with the lines, 'yet of all the words / we knew, his name was the most dear. / We give thanks he was spoken here.'

Frank leaves his poem unfinished.

Don in a grey jumper in the café at the Fruitmarket Gallery trying to insist that this meeting was purely pastoral, that I didn't need to keep talking about my thesis.

Don telling me about his dad, his mum.

Don outside the back entrance to Waverley, hugging me goodbye in the October chill.

Don in the café at the National Portrait Gallery in high summer, me in a green camisole so that I can show off the new tattoo on the back of my left upper arm. Don saying, 'Sean tells me you're in love.'

Don in his old flat, four of us sat around the fruit bowl drinking black coffee & reading poems. I walk home across Bruntsfield Links & the Meadows & feel like a gull on the air currents.

Don checking in.

Don in his new flat, mercilessly beating me at pool.

A text that says *Do you know how Don's getting on? I heard something about tests?* & I am on a train & it feels as though the carriage floor has blinked out of existence.

Weeks later & he's fine but I have learned what they mean by substitute father figure & it means that a train no longer has a floor you can rely on & the rushing tracks are just waiting for that slippage.

Later: a summer where Don is on the phone almost every day & I sit in what was once my father's study, making brutal, hacking edits to my thesis, a thousand words at a time. Moss, convalescing, deadheads the roses for my mother & brings me an accidentally-lopped healthy bud in a little glass for the spartan desk. Don groans performatively every time I tell him my wordcount. A hard, hardened July, but every day some form of laughter echoes out from my father's old study.

I dream that I am cruel to someone who is making a phone call to comfort a grieving friend. I tell her "everyone dies" when she protests. We are in a huge country estate that is also maybe an Oxbridge college. In every painting there is a cameo of Caroline Calloway that I am convinced she has painted in herself. I run around from room to room finding them & being mean to people.

The comforter & I are waitresses or possibly poetry festival organisers. Either way a huge trestle table covered in roast beef & small pickles has been set up & as I try to apologise the comforter becomes the griever. She asks which pool I have access to & I laugh & say something patronising about class because she is bourgeois. Whenever I try to apologise someone interrupts to talk about the beef.

In the dream my father is still alive but I use his death as an excuse anyway. I tell her grief made me a bitch & I wake up in the creaking dark still trying to justify this.

I would like to say that grief makes you a narcissist but I am writing during a pandemic & I don't want to say that *in these unprecedented times*

so let me say that I am a narcissist & my grief is narcissistic

do you know anything about my father yet?

memoir, traditionally, was supposed to be a form used to lionise the dead

memoir was supposed to be about the subject not The Subject

my father is the void at the centre of this book

my father is the negative space in Ólafur Eliasson's *The presence of absence pavilion* (2019), which you can walk right into, taking the place of the glacial ice around which the bronze was cast

we like to put ourselves in the middle of things, to inhabit spaces made for others & consider ourselves at home

I haven't told you anything about my father yet

all I can conjure is the white of his wrist next to the perennial watch strap tan line

as if that can stand for the whole absent presence of the man

as if that strip of rarely-seen flesh can say how he felt about his skin, the body he lived in

my not-really godmother Helen once told me (mortified, fourteen) that *he has really great legs, your father, for a man*

I don't know if he felt that about his legs

I know that he once shaved his face clean, the first year we went to Cornwall, in the middle of the holiday only in writing this do I realise that he picked then because the only people that would see him were us

plus, holiday exuberance (what I understood it to be at the time)

it was an experiment, no one liked it

but maybe he did, maybe he had a whole relationship with his short, neat facial hair that I was never privy to

maybe it formed part of his understanding of his selfhood the way I know it does for people who do not occupy the space "father" to me

other bodily memories: the thing he used to do with his thumb & forefinger that made a tissue paper noise (dry skin?); shirts tucked in, t-shirts left out; the gesture of him flattening his hair down at the front; the time I bit him near his armpit while playfighting when I was four (in my head there is an immediate huge purple welt of a bruise, which is not possible, but I still feel guilty about it); the way he blew his nose (endlessly) into a handkerchief, & the old-fashioned idiosyncracy of it; the sound of his fingers drumming on the steering wheel & the thud of the hard pats he gave the dog

I am trying to remember what a hug from him felt like but it's gone already which is awful awful

like trying to hold negative space, to mould yourself to something fundamentally not there

recast the bronze & the shape comes out wrong

twisted or blunted or dented in the wrong places

too soft, too hard, reduced to tiny details

I want to list Christmas gifts: annual subscription to Wisden, Alan Johnson autobiography, slippers, endless cheap reading glasses in bright colours, DVD of Blackpool FC season highlights, Molton Brown "smellies," Amy MacDonald album to list beloved objects: battered and sun-bleached Loveless Cafe baseball cap, Glad to Be Gray badge, navy towelling dressing-gown (have I merged it with yours?), Blackpool scarf, Guggenheim Bilbao t-shirt, faintly embarrassing Barack Obama HOPE poster on the door of his study, cricket bat

& yet all of this is just more bronze

melt it down, cast it again

write about the angelic black & white photograph under my grandparents' kitchen pass, all straight fair hair & side parting & photo day scrubbed face

write about the teenager in sandals that match his father's, clutching a brand new camera in a brown leather case, on holiday in Blackpool or Torquay

write about the young man in little white shorts & plimsolls & socks pulled up (*Moss: I love this outfit!*), shaggy 70s hair, leaning against a wall in the sun

something always pleasantly effeminate about my father

but I don't know these people, never did

only ever the rounded belly version, the greyer hair, the scritchier beard

the silver ring my mother bought him on their first holiday together that he never took off

& that she now wears on her (I suppose) widow's hand

the trace it leaves; the shadow of one body moved to another

they had to resize it for her

someone melting down the metal a bit, so that what fit him now fits her

the space inside it not quite, exactly, what it really was

Moss is fascinated by dreams. He recounts his own to me almost every morning, and occasionally attends the Queer Dreaming Matrix, a Jungian project that sounds horrifying to me in both theory and practice. What do I care about other people's symbologies?

[my entire politic dissolves in the face of grief, I suppose // suddenly: fuck the communal, I am alone & adrift & want nothing & will give nothing]

My own dreams, for the most part, blink out of mind immediately upon waking. Clearly I have no use for them; indistinct, orangey, slinking things. Either that, or I simply do not dream.

Except, sometimes— when I wake with a gasping feeling, like all that wuthering has come home to roost, & the bed tips & I am full, truly saturated, with rage or fear or something less nameable, & after this passes there is just some *image*, some benighted gif, spooling out & back & out again.

Me & my family are in blue-grey tube rings in an underground cavern. It is dank & cold, but we are definitely On Holiday. My father, who in real life could not swim, is there, but always just out of frame. My sister & I are fighting about how the other one is always on her phone too much. My mother is just about to intervene when my sister says look, Daddy's here right now, we have to be here right now *& I shoot out my hand, quick-fast, & put it in her mouth, scrabbling my fingers around like a jellyfish.*

We did have one last holiday. Perfect, because we didn't know it would be the last. Didn't know he had three months. Didn't even know he was sick. Hot sun & tiles around the pool & crickets at night, the works. The four of us watching the moon change position each night from the terrace.

The last time I saw him, I had gone home to Leeds after he was discharged from hospital the first? second? time. I don't remember much of it, don't like to hold those images in my head. He was pale & too thin & he was tired a lot. I was due to get an early train back up to Edinburgh, so on the last night, before he went to bed (slowly, early), I said goodnight. We were stood in the hallway & I hugged him & he afterwards he held my shoulders & looked at me & told me how proud he was. His voice cracked — not unusually (*silly, soppy man*, as my mother used to say) — & I shook my head & shrugged off the compliment, laughing. We did the standard *night night/ sleep well/love you* bit that we've all done since I was a child, though the usual *see you in the morning* at the end was missing.

A few days before he died, I called him whilst I was in the supermarket — the little ScotMid on Leith Walk — juggling the phone against my ear whilst I grabbed things off the shelves. He was in the hospital, & just wanted to hear about my life. I told him about my first foray into teaching undergrads, the lesson plans & my nerves & how much I enjoyed it. I asked how he was & I don't remember the answer. This, presumably, was when we discussed the Yorkshire puddings that I was going to make. I realised I had timed my phone call badly because I actually needed to go & pay, & told him this, & we said things like *talk soon* & *look after yourself* & *love you*.

Everyone said, later, that it was better that way. Better that we never had to have some forced ideal last moment, that we just talked & loved each other & then that was it.

And I think *but that was it*.

It has snowed twice since you died.

I didn't even notice the first time. I mean, I noticed the now, & that he had died, but not the fact of it being the first snow that I'd ever seen that he hadn't.

(This is, of course, to take blatant liberties with artistic license — I haven't lived with my father for ten years &, never mind trips taken apart, the difference in microclimate between Yorkshire & Scotland would probably account for at least a flake of something seen by me & not by him.)

But this time I am noticing. It's the dry kind that creaks under boots & is blue on the side hit by the leftover Christmas lights on Rose Street.

Hey Vati, I am very happy; I like the snow, cold in my throat, & I like to walk home alone at night through a city that feels like it belongs to me. I am not interested in timelessness, placelessness. It is March 2018 in Edinburgh; the snow is the Beast from the East & I am less than a month away from meeting the love of my life. The streets have that quiet clamour of unexpected, unseasonal snow — & it's perhaps too often cited to be interesting (o to be interesting), but it's true that the grim trappings of self-conscious adulthood loosen slightly (a young woman in a sensible dove-grey wrap coat almost knocks her friend off her sharp little heels with a well-aimed handful, & two teenage boys without coats laugh as if in comradeship with her — no agenda, no threat).

Yanis Varoufakis has just published a book called *Talking to My Daughter About the Economy* & I am seeing it displayed everywhere. My father was an economist — a labour market expert with a Labour Party membership card almost as old as he was & a Blackpool FC season ticket older than that. The cover of Varoufakis' book is Blackpool FC tangerine — the colour of our living room for many years (unrelated, my mother always insisted).

& to think, I never normally know what to get you for Christmas.

He is not here to explain to me the difference between the single market & the customs union & it seems increasingly important that I know.

Hey Vati, I joined a trade union.

Last semester I missed teaching some of my classes because you were dying (& then died). This semester we are on strike & I am tired but when we sing Billy Bragg you are there in the North Sea wind & the snow on the picket.

(even though you could never sing)

(& you didn't teach me the old union hymns)

It has snowed a lot more since I began writing this & I am going to lose count soon.

I have so many more things to tell you.

It is Kim Kardashian West's 40th birthday & we are all about to find out what you get a woman valued at $800million.

Yeah, we're ready.

Okay!

Kim, this is from Kanye, happy fortieth!

Kim tucks up her legs into a plastic chair pushed against a blank wall, as the lights go out.

Is it a light show? I'm scared, is anyone gonna jump out at me?

From the blueish darkness, a shape, a voice.

Happy birthday, Kimberley.

A shift in lighting, & there he is: cream suit, pompadour hair, looking like he walked out of one of their famous, on-brand home videos.

Look at you, you're forty and all grown up.

Only, a little off. Skin too shiny, neck a touch too long, hand gestures on a kind of loop.

You look beautiful, just like when you were a little girl.

Robert Kardashian died eighteen years ago. Kim, Kourt, Khloé: famously bereaved. Kim of the dead dad. The thing money can never buy back.

I watch over you, and your sisters and brother, and the kids every day, he says, as if to get it out of the way.

Until now? No. The hologram is horrifying, ghoulish. These people bought up uncanny valley years ago, but as the lights go up two full minutes later (*Don't forget to say your prayers!*) there is a ghastly silence. The resurrected image of her father has — in a particularly Baudrillardian touch — dissolved into Disney-style sparkles and been whisked away, leaving just the strangely blank room. The only sound is a set of little gasping sobs.

Kim, I want to say, *grief is an Agnes Martin painting. It is an affectless blank we must square up to, lose ourselves in. Kim,* I want to say, *trace the lines, find the edges of your feelings, let them fall off the sides of the canvas. Mark time in the boxes, the creamgreybluebeige variation. It's slight, but it's there, & you can have it. Stagger of penstroke, sudden duckeggporcelainsky, rigidity of spine, of box-for-ball, the decision to be fine.*

Kim, I want to say, *flatness is your friend. Get out of the hyperreal. Me & Agnes have got you.*

But who am I to judge? To look to Agnes instead of a hologram?

For about eight years, maybe 1989 to 1997, my Grandpa, my dad's dad, was obsessed with his video camera. Brought it everywhere, filmed everything. My mother, who has a horror of her own image being captured that is not dissimilar to that of early subjects' fear of the daguerrotype as a method of soul-stealing, hated it. So she doesn't appear that much in the shelf's worth of VHS tapes, constantly dodging the shot. Me & my dad, and later my baby sister, are the stars.

After my father died, the tapes — which had sat forgotten in the cellar for years — were suddenly precious treasure. For months my mother looked into ways of converting them into something we could watch again, finally finding a nice man who would make them into DVDs for an extortionate price.

The tapes were a kind of grail for me. Long-promised, inaccessible, a mythic object, I put all of my hopes for resurrection into them.

Early on, my mother said to me & my sister: *don't let him become your "sainted father."* I don't know if this seemed particularly profound to her at the time, but it has stuck with me as a kind of mantra over the past few years.

Ever since I met Moss, I have been trying to introduce my father to him. I remember walking through The Meadows on an early date, sighing performatively at the sight of amateur cricketers in their whites, hurling spinballs at each other. He asked, and I answered, recounting youthful summer Saturdays (Sundays? bank holidays?) spent driving to tiny English villages to set up a picnic of sausage rolls and carrot sticks and not-really-watch my dad's team lose good-naturedly. The oven fan turns itself off finally, halfway through tea, and I tell him how my father would always sigh at this point, saying *that's better*, settling into his chair. I tell him about the way he and I would always put our apple stickers on our noses, how that tightness on the bridge of my nose still feels like comfort, like the best joke ever. I tell him about all the ways they are alike, their shared soppiness, the way so many people mistake them for serious, the absurdity of that to those that love them. When I tell him about the way my dad would help himself to seconds at teatime on the basis that 'I've got mi balance wrong' (the Wool in him popping up briefly), he picks up the phrase, says it so regularly, so unconsciously that sometimes I forget he never heard the original.

I try to tell Moss the silly things, the unbeautiful things, the very small.

This is what I was looking for in the tapes. A reel of footage that would elucidate a whole person for Moss; would say *behold, the man,* in all his normal comprehensible glory, & lo, you will understand him entirely, & therefore my family & therefore me. You will see gentleness beyond compare, you will see the way he "took to fatherhood like a duck to water" as everyone said, you will see every terrible joke he ever told & all the times I rolled my childish eyes & called him silly & all the times he said *oh okay would you like me to be a serious daddy instead then* & held a boring face for— how long? it always felt like forever. You will see how he thought my mother the most brilliant person in the world, genuinely couldn't understand his own greater success, with the sweet but frustrating blinkeredness of the— what? post-patriarch? You will see everything he was to me, to us, & us to him, & it will be like you knew him.

Instead, of course, we watch a few hours of my grandfather filming animals at Knowsley Safari Park. The camera zooms past my father to the lions in their cuddle puddle, the monkeys on the bonnet in the rain (the 90s!) & occasionally to me & my sister in the back seat for comment. I am about 7, & this is the most recent of the tapes. The closest to the man I remember.

After: a pub garden somewhere on the Wirral with one of those adventure playgrounds. Grandpa, a picnic bench paparazzo, trying to catch a shot of me unsuccessfully navigating a set of swinging logs on chains. I am painfully shy at this age, self-conscious & easily humiliated, yet always wanting to be perceived. Other children are objects of fascination & terror, but I want to be liked. My father, like a voiceover, *ah, she's found a friend, we won't see her for hours now. She plays with all these kids up at the caravan, you know — it's so good for her self-confidence.*

And there, this is enough. Moss turns & I see that he understands that I was so loved.

[Before Septimus & Rezia & Regent's Park & Evans & 'feeling very little and very reasonably,' or perhaps really at the exact same time as all that, we follow Woolf, trailing after Peter Walsh down the park's broad paths as he remembers Clarissa & Sally & Bourton & all that lost youth &—

It was awful, he cried, awful, awful!

Still, the sun was hot. Still, one got over things. Still, life had a way of adding day to day.]

It is 2020 & it is the earliest arrival of spring in a century.

A man covered in red paint puts on a pair of safety goggles & drives a red toy pickup into the first of a chain of dominoes. Silence, as domino hits domino & domino tugs string & string starts second toy car down ramp to billiard ball & billiard ball hits vinyl which pulls thread & a brightly coloured lever swings down to start a drumbeat & someone sings *you know you can't keep letting it get you down / and you can't keep dragging that dead weight around* & things keep moving.

I watch videos of Rube Goldberg machines, one after another. The feeling of process, of progress, is immensely satisfying to me. The endless forward motion, this to this, the constant producing of effects. (*It is the earliest arrival of spring in a century.*) I love doing the laundry for this reason; even when you're not really *doing* it, it's still happening: the spin cycle works away while you listen to podcasts, stare at your emails. The last load is always drier than it was five minutes ago.

This, perhaps, is the thing I like about plants, too. You don't have to be doing anything for them to keep growing, they just do. New leaf unfurling, roots pushing into mulch, imperceptible lengthening of stems, growth for no reason whatsoever. I didn't make it happen, but I can somehow claim it. Progress. The constant feeling that things will get better, that wounds are closing over, the body repairing itself, the processes we rely on. Spring.

When the morning comes / When the morning comes / Let it go, this too shall pass / Let it go, this too shall pass / When the morning comes

At home among my own snack bowls where I'm supposed to be I read Chen Chen's poem about shitting & loving someone & I have been awake since a nightmare wrenched me from the duvet at 3am (Bot 12, whomst I thought was my friend, put a pillow over my face) & so I get a lump in my throat that the snacks can't get past & add the song 'Married in Vegas' to my playlist for you.

A woman on a podcast says: you do not have what you used to have, that is all grief is.

Alexa and I do 13,000 steps, walking in circles around the cemetery near our tenements.

We walk in the tracks of cars that have trundled round the paths in search of a particular grave at which to pay their respects.

I walk in the left track & Lex walks in the right track (slightly less than two metres apart) & the frozen mud is spongy beneath our boots & we are both furious because our fathers died & other people are wrong about grief.

I dream that there is a face at the door.

It is our flat but not our flat because the door has panels of glass that our door does not have.

Through one of these panels looks a face.

In my dream I look at the face for a long time. A round, white man's face. Friendly, soft, fringed in grey fuzz.

After a while, I begin to panic, because this is my father's face & I no longer recognise it.

For the next few days, Springsteen's 'I'll See You In My Dreams' plays in my head on repeat (*up around the river bend / for death is not the end*), even though it is inconceivable to me that there are such things as new (& newer & newer & newer) Springsteen albums.

I go back to 'Terry's Song' & try to remember his face, while fat sloppy tears ruin the varnish of my little desk.

also the plant called 'regret,' of which there are two kinds, one with a flower like that of a larkspur, the other not coloured but white, which is used at funerals; and this one lasts longer.

Butler, again, writes that '[p]erhaps, rather, one mourns when one accepts that by the loss one undergoes one will be changed, possible for ever. Perhaps mourning has to do with agreeing to undergo a transformation (perhaps one should say *submitting* to a transformation) the full result of which one cannot know in advance.'

When C.S. Lewis opens *A Grief Observed* with the idea that grief feels like fear, I know what he means, in that it's the same as I felt when I was evacuating my bowels so continuously in those first few days and weeks. Only I, perhaps poisoned by oversimplified therapeutic language and the pathologisation of emotion, would call this Anxiety.

I accept, in that I know my father is dead. But Butler's right to say *submitting* because I do not want the transformation that comes with loss. Still, I am anxious. Still, I reject it.

This morning I woke up to a text from my mother that said *Please ring when you get this message* and we all know what a text like that means.

Our family dog, arthritic and confused and increasingly neurotic, was just too distressed by a world that didn't make sense to him any more. Could barely walk, was up all night every night. It was time.

It all comes back. I sit in the fat armchair that Moss and I carried home from the British Heart Foundation furniture shop at the bottom of Leith Walk, bickering the entire way about how to effectively carry 30 kilos of bulky paisley chair. The chair rewards me, anchoring me in its fat arms as I drown in immediate aftermath.

From the other room: a girl in a zoom call with a hundred people sobs

I say, *what the fuck was that about*

Moss says, *she'd lost someone, she was grieving*

I say, *that's completely fucking unacceptable behaviour, it's so selfish*

Moss says, *Rosa she's grieving*

I say, *so is everyone*

I say, *why is this the one thing we let people get away with*

I say, *people let you get away with anything when you're grieving, it's pathetic*

I say, *god it's so fucking embarrassing, why don't people have more shame*

Moss says, *other people seemed affected, they were crying too*

I say, *not out of sympathy for her, they have their own shit, they feel sorry for themselves*

Moss says, *maybe they did feel sympathy, it was very sad*

I say, *pathetic*

later, to Alexa, I say, *people are going to say the same about me & my stupid book*

I say, *I don't even care about my stupid grief any more*

I think, *pathetic*

Butler (a final time): 'I am not sure I know when mourning is successful, or when one has fully mourned another human being.'

Dear Alexa,

I've seen just about every available version of Sondheim's *Into the Woods*, and the 1987 Broadway cast is the best. Well, no, I take that back. Elements of others are better: Vanessa Williams' costuming and Judi Dench as the Giant in the 2002 Broadway revival, something about Meryl Streep's blue hair and Emily Blunt's face in the 2014 film — and the 2010 Regent's Park Open Air Theatre production, in which the casting of the Narrator changes everything. But everything (as you know & as always) hinges on the Witch. And nothing comes close to Bernadette Peters.

In Act I she's by turns hilarious and pathetic, pausing with farcical melodrama before jabbing her knobbly walking stick at the empty womb of the Baker's Wife (*nothing cooking in there now, is there?*), and desperately reaching out to Rapunzel, who turns from her (*you are ashamed of me, you are ashamed*). And then in Act II — in Act II she's beautiful and terrible in purple velvet, holding her finger up to her lips as everyone rounds on her, moving upstage en masse as she stands stock still, staring down at them all with perfect, unmoved contempt. *It's the last midnight, it's the boom, squish*, she sings slowly, turning to watch her own hand curl around the deeply sexy *squish*. She glitters malevolently, turning on the other characters, pointing out their foibles, their failings.

And then, with arms folded and dripping with disdain—

You're so nice / You're not good / you're not bad / you're just nice / I'm not good / I'm not nice / I'm just right / I'm the Witch / you're the world

The Witch is a role that lives and dies by its strength. It's too easy to play her as bitter, as cold and warped and abandoned. In this moment, Bernadette Peters is electric with power; you can see it coming off the ends of her glorious hair, shimmering from her crappy Hallowe'en costume red cloak. She's the *world*.

It's slightly earlier, though, that she begins to flex her muscles, to extricate herself from the mire of other people's feelings, from her own awful, twisted grief. The Baker's Wife dies offstage somewhere, and Chip Zein as the Baker clutches at her scarf — desperate remnant, all he has left.

Baker: I should have insisted that she stay home, I—
Witch: Remorse will get you nowhere.
Baker: My wife is *dead*!
Witch: WAKE. UP. People are dying all around you, you're not the only one to suffer a loss. [pause] When you're dead, you're dead.
[the audience laughs]

I don't know why I'm telling you this really, except to say that I have been Baker and Witch and often both in one day. No day the same. No grief the same.

Sometimes people leave you / halfway through the wood, says Sondheim. He always adds, though: *you are not alone / no one is alone*.

Sometimes the best I can do is to say that grief is an Agnes Martin painting.

'To Hell With It,' says Frank, still grieving his unfinished grief, his unfinished friend.

       nothing now can be changed, as if
                       last crying no tears will dry
  and Bunny never change her writing

I wanted to put it all in here. To build a small green monument to my grief & to be able to feel I'd said it all. Got it all in, every touchstone of my being all neatly filtered through grief & houseplants. Very good, very clever. Enough art, enough critical theory, enough words from other people to make it all sound good.

Joan Didion constantly repeats (she loves to quote herself) her approach to mourning: 'Read, learn, work it up, go to the literature. Information is control.'

I only read Didion to write this. Her & C.S. Lewis & Max Porter & all the other literatures of loss. I only read them to write about them. I never went to the literature. I didn't want information.

About a year after he died I started a kind of journal in my Notes app. Slowly it became something outside myself & I wanted to put my whole self in it.

But it is three years since he died, & counting, & there is too much to think about. My original pothos has moved six or eight times through the flat, & its longest vines hit the overcrowded floor of the living room & turn up again. It needs pinning up — along the walls, maybe, over the picture frames — but I never get round to it. Its propagated baby is now the size & shape of the ur-pothos I had tattooed on the back of my left arm in the summer of 2018.

I had drawn it on the back of an archive call slip from the Houghton Library at Harvard, in a tiny airless room in a bizarre AirBnB in Cambridge, Massachusetts, drinking the last of the four sour beers from the Stop & Shop across the freeway. I had spent a month walking across the Massachussetts Turnpike to the Breakfast Club diner or the Dunkin' or the 7/11 to get a colossal iced coffee with half-and-half, before plodding on through the shimmering blank heat across the Charles River to the cool atrium & Meka the security guard, my only friend, who would smile & raise his eyebrows if I got there after ten. There I would spend the day carefully turning the leaves of Bunny Lang's teenage diaries, her tissue-paper manuscripts, photographing, reading draft after draft of mad, forgotten poems, photographing, turning, requesting the next box, gentle gentle.

Every day I wanted to call my father, tell him about this strange life of Americana, tell him that I knew I got my love of it from him, tell him that I knew him, that he knew me.

It was awful, he cried, awful, awful!
        Still, the sun was hot. Still, one got over things. Still, life had a way of adding day to day.

When I came home, my pothos was almost dead & so it seemed the right time to get out the call slip & put it on me forever.

I don't want to say *I brought it back to life* because it sounds like a stupid metaphor, but I brought it back to life & it wasn't a metaphor. It was a real growing thing that I could claim: a triumph.

All this to say: I can't put it all in.

All this to say: my father died & for a while my houseplants seemed to have something to say about it.

All this to say: things keep growing. Things keep dying. The vines keep getting longer & a book can only be so long.

And yet. And yet and yet and still and still.

Works Cited

WRITING

Adichie, Chimamanda Ngozi. 'Notes on Grief'. *The New Yorker* (10 September 2020)

Ariès, Philippe. *Western Attitudes Towards Death from the Middle Ages to the Present* (Johns Hopkins, 1974)
— — —. *The Hour of Our Death* (trans. Helen Weaver) (Knopf, 1981)

Baudrillard, Jean. *Simulacra and Simulation* (University of Michigan Press, 1994)
— — —. *America* (Verso, 2010)

Butler, Judith. *Precarious Life: The Powers of Mourning and Violence* (Verso, 2004)

Chee, Alexander. 'The Rosary' from *How to Write an Autobiographical Novel* (Bloomsbury, 2018)

Chen, Chen. 'Winter'. *Poetry* (July/August 2017)

Coolidge, Susan M. *What Katy Did* (Parragon Books, 1993)

Cummings, E.E. '[i carry your heart with me(i carry it in]' from *Complete Poems, 1904-1962* (Liveright, 2016)

Didion, Joan. *The Year of Magical Thinking* (Harper Perennial, 2006)

Freud, Sigmund. 'Mourning and Melancholia'. *The Standard Edition of the Complete Psychological Works of Sigmund Freud. Volume XIV (1914-1916).* Trans. James Strachey (Random House, 2001)

Glück, Louise. 'Vespers' from *The Wild Iris* (Ecco Press, 1992)

LeSueur, Joe, *Digressions on Some Poems by Frank O'Hara: A Memoir* (Farrar, Straus & Giroux, 2003)

Lewis, C.S. *A Grief Observed* (Faber & Faber, 2013)

Moore, Chadwick. 'New York's most popular plant can kill you and your pets'. *New York Post* (15 December 2016)

Nelson, Maggie. *Women, the New York School, and Other True Abstractions* (University of Iowa Press, 2007)
— — —. *The Red Parts: Autobiography of a Trial* (Vintage, 2017)

Nonnus. *Dionysiaca*. Trans. W.H.D. Rouse (Harvard University Press, 1940)

Notley, Alice. *The Descent of Alette* (Penguin, 1996)
— — —. *Coming After: Essays on Poetry* (University of Michigan Press, 2005)

O'Hara, Frank. 'To the Mountains in New York'; 'Song of Ending'; 'A Step Away From Them'; 'The Unfinished' and 'To Hell With It' from *Collected Poems* (University of California Press, 1971)
— — —. 'Entombment' and 'To Dick' from *Poems Retrieved* (City Lights, 2013)

Paterson, Don. 'Funeral Prayer' from *40 Sonnets* (Faber & Faber, 2015)

Porter, Max. *Grief is the Thing with Feathers* (Faber & Faber, 2016)

Riley, Denise. 'Wherever You Are, Be Somewhere Else' from *Selected Poems* (2000)

Rilke, Rainer Maria. 'Archaic Torso of Apollo' from *Ahead of All Parting: The Selected Poetry and Prose of Rainer Maria Rilke*. Ed. Trans. Stephen Mitchell (Random House, 1996)

Roosevelt, Theodore, *Personal diary of Theodore Roosevelt, 1884*, Theodore Roosevelt Papers, Library of Congress Manuscript Division, Theodore Roosevelt Digital Library, Dickinson State University

Plato. Volume IV: *Cratylus. Parmenides. Greater Hippias. Lesser Hippias*. Trans. Harold North Fowler. (Loeb, 1926)

Seneca. 'De Consolatione ad Helviam'. *Dialogues and Letters*. Trans. C.D.N. Costa. (Penguin, 1997)

Theophrastus. *Enquiry into plants and minor works on odours and weather signs*. Trans. Arthur Hort (Heinemann, 1916)

Woolf, Virginia, *Mrs Dalloway* (Vintage, 2004)

Wright, James. 'Lying in a Hammock at William Duffy's Farm in Pine Island, Minnesota' from *Above the River: The Complete Poems and Selected Prose* (Wesleyan University Press, 1990)

ART

Anonymous. *A man stabbing a woman with a stiletto*. Wellcome Collection, London (18—.)

Bosch, Hieronymus (after), *The Garden of earthly delights*. Wellcome Collection, London (between 1500 and 1599)

Curtius, Philippe. *Sleeping Beauty*. The Metropolitan Museum, New York (1989, after 1765 original)

Eliasson, Ólafur. *The presence of absence pavilion*. Tate Modern, London (2019)

Martin, Agnes. *Night Sea*. SFMOMA, San Francisco (1963)
———. *Stars*. Solomon R. Guggenheim Museum, New York (1963)

———. *The Peach*. Pippy Houldworth Gallery, London (1964)
———. *Morning*. Tate Modern, London (1965)
———. *On a Clear Day* (portfolio). MoMA, New York (1973)
———. *Faraway Love*. Tate Modern, London (1999)

McCarthy, Paul. *Paul Dreaming, Vertical, Horizontal*. The Metropolitan Museum, New York (2005-2012)

Smith, Chloë. *Holding It Together*: 'It Goes On' with Jassy Earl (2020)

MUSIC, THEATRE, TELEVISION

Beethoven, Ludwig van. Symphony No. 9 in D Minor, Op. 125 "Choral": IV. Presto: *Ode to Joy* (1822-1824)

'Shadow.' *Buffy the Vampire Slayer*, created by Joss Whedon. Season 5, Episode 8. Mutant Enemy Productions (2000)

Cave, Nick, & the Bad Seeds. 'Into My Arms.' *The Boatman's Call* (Mute/Reprise, 1997)

Foundations, The. 'Build Me Up Buttercup'. *Build Me Up Buttercup* (PYE, 1968)

OK Go. 'This Too Shall Pass' (video). Dirs. James Frost, OK Go, Syyn Labs (2010)

Sondheim, Stephen. *Into the Woods*. Dir. James Lapine. Martin Beck Theatre, New York (1987)

Springsteen, Bruce. 'Terry's Song'. *Magic* (Columbia, 2007)
———. 'Tucson Train'. *Western Stars* (Columbia, 2019)
———. 'I'll See You in My Dreams'. *Letter to You* (Columbia, 2020)

Acknowledgements

An extract from this work, in an earlier version, was longlisted for the Ivan Juritz Prize for Creative Experiment in 2019, and I would like to thank the Judges — Richard Scott, Jeremy Harding, and Rachel Cusk — for their generous consideration and encouragement.

I am incredibly grateful to Aaron Kent and the team at Broken Sleep Books, for their seemingly boundless patience and their faith in this work (and, yikes, me).

I would also like to thank everyone who finds themself named in the pages of this book; you appear here as a testament to all the various & varied ways a person can find community, companionship and solace. I consider myself incredibly lucky, in particular, to have the love and friendship of Holly Edwards, E Jamieson, Claire Stewart, Bella Phillips, Rosie Robertson (who also create the beautiful cover image), Patrick Errington, Justin Duff, and Don Paterson.

Regular, repeated, and eternal thanks are also due to my mother, Janie Percy-Smith, and my sister Christina.

Above all, I am grateful to Alexa Winik, Becky Birrell, and Moss Pepe, the first readers of this book and chief reasons it exists in any kind of finished form. I love you, and blame you entirely for it not remaining safely in my Notes app forever.

LAY OUT YOUR UNREST